THE   JAPANESE   WAY
WITH   FLOWERS

Books by RACHEL CARR

STEPPING STONES TO JAPANESE FLORAL ART

JAPANESE FLORAL ART: Symbolism, Cult and Practice

A YEAR OF FLOWERS

HOURS AND FLOWERS

THE PICTURE STORY OF JAPAN

THE JAPANESE WAY
WITH FLOWERS

by RACHEL E. CARR

ILLUSTRATIONS BY ALAIN R. CARR

Harper & Row, Publishers · New York and London

FIRST EDITION

LIBRARY OF CONGRESS CATALOG CARD NUMBER: 65–14678

Contents

PART II 24 BASIC DESIGNS WITH STEP-BY-STEP INSTRUCTIONS

Author's Note

The purpose of this book is to give the flower arranger of the Western world a practical knowledge of Japan's rich and creative floral art. It is planned as a primer, and can also be used as an instruction guide.

The simplicity of the arrangements selected makes them suited to the decor of Occidental homes. The designs are not static. Each can be re-created with a variety of flowers, branches, and foliage. Suggestions for variations are given with each design and permit freedom of selection to harmonize with one's own environment.

A broad classification of popular seasonal plants used in flower arrangement appears in the appendix. It will be most helpful in identifying the different types of plants and possible substitutes for designs. The new gardener who may wish to grow such plants for use in flower arrangement will find the classification helpful.

To acquire maximum pleasure from this book it should be read first for some understanding of the philosophy, symbolism, history, and design principles of this age-old art. Once these unique characteristics of the Japanese way with flowers have become familiar to you, your imagination will be spurred to individual creative designing.

The charcoal illustrations in this book were done by my 20-year-old son, Alain, whose childhood years were spent in China and Japan.

New York   —RACHEL CARR
January 1965

PART I

Flowers have an expression of countenance as much as men or animals. Some seem to smile; some have a sad expression; some are pensive and diffident; others again are plain, honest and upright. . . .

—Henry Ward Beecher

1 Ikebana —
The Art of Japanese Flower Arrangement

THE JAPANESE are an artistic nation. They have a deep grasp of aesthetics and creative vision that seems inherent in their way of life. This is the reason their floral art is unique. Through understanding of the laws of form in art they produce fine qualities of linear perspective, balance, and spacing in their flower arrangements. With only a handful of flowers, branches, or foliage the Japanese are able to create designs of compelling beauty which express the relation of art to nature. No other country has achieved a similar artistic plateau.

Ikebana is an ancient art.* Its roots trace back to the sixth century, when the offering of flowers to Buddha in the temples was an integral part of daily ritual. From these religious beginnings ikebana has developed into a rich and highly cultivated art encompassing a variety of styles—from early classical, emulating nature, to contemporary modern, free of imposed formulas.

Flower arrangers of the Western world can borrow profitably from the subtleties of Japanese design. In re-

* *Ikebana* (ee-KEH-bah-nah) has become a universal word. Its accepted translation is Japanese flower arrangement.

cent years Japanese influence has become quite apparent in the modern decor of Occidental living. The illusion of space and avoidance of symmetry are applied effectively to both indoor decorating and landscaping. Japanese use of linear rhythm has been successfully adapted to the popular Western "line arrangements." Much more, however, can be learned from the Japanese ability to create with few lines strong emotional qualities expressing elements of movement that vibrate with rhythm.

Words like *shibui* (she-bu-yee), *wabi* (wah-bee), and *sabi* (sah-bee) are becoming familiar expressions in the Western world. Shibui is the final criterion for the ultimate in beauty. Wabi implies a discriminating taste for simplicity and refinement, and sabi connotes the highest praise for an object patinated by use and time. If we look for these descriptive terms in ikebana they can be found in the Japanese awareness of nature brought into subtle play. Compositions depict seasonal changes, plants in their natural environment, and the dramatization of a particular tree or flower. The Japanese make great use of tonal shadings and irregular patterns found in nature. There is unexpected appeal in a gnarled branch covered with moss or lichen used to symbolize an aged tree. Patina on a craggy bark in a rustic woodland, and smooth water-washed stones amid aquatic plants as part of a quiet pond scene, add charm and imaginative realism. A sensitive balance is kept between the spiritual and the realistic.

SYMBOLISM AND PHILOSOPHY

The Japanese have a romantic attitude toward nature. Many plants of the floral kingdom are endowed with exotic titles. The "four aristocrats" are the plum, bamboo, chrysanthemum, and orchid; the "gentleman among flowers" is the lotus. Maple, peony, cherry, narcissus, and iris are flowers of "princely descent." Some classical designs are given poetically symbolic names such as Waxing Moon, Waning Moon, and Full Moon; Junk Resting at Anchor, or Junk Far Out at Sea; Profile of Mount Fuji, and Water Diving Plum.

The traditional styles are built on an unequal or scalene triangle, adapted from an ancient Chinese concept that the symbolic triad divides the universe into three realms: heaven, earth, and humanity. The triad is embellished with philosophical symbolism. The two cosmic forces, negative and positive, represent the law of contrast. *In* is the negative and *Yo*, the positive. This balance of opposites precludes monotony of composition. It is apparent in the use of light and dark colors, left and right curves, weak and strong elements, and the different stages of plant growth.

The principle of "hill-plain-water" represents levels of perspective. Branches symbolize a mountain or hill; flowers, the plain or valley; aquatic plants, a stream or water. This principle is also expressed as: distance, middle ground, and foreground.

It is from this rich cultural store that Japan's contemporary flower masters have drawn inspiration to achieve new depths and media in the changing artistic environment of their life. The heritage of the past is invisibly embedded in the modern floral styles, which are evocative rather than symbolic. They inspire individual thought and emotion, and reveal an inherent understanding of dynamics in modern design.

The Japanese have a sense of fitness, and the unique ability to assimilate native and foreign influences. Although Japan's culture stems from China, today it is a country with two civilizations—East and West, merging as one.

IKEBANA—A SERIOUS STUDY
AND WAY OF LIFE

Ikebana is deeply associated with the Japanese way of life. Interest in this art is so intense that competition is keen among the thousands of Japanese flower schools. Of this large number many are branches within branches of prominent national schools. Faced with the challenge of the progressively modern schools, traditional flower masters of the "old school" now adapt their curricula to include the popular contemporary styles and modifications of the formalized classical styles.

The famous exponents of ikebana are men. These flower masters devote their lives to the constant pursuit of new dimensions, adding to the breadth and depth of this expressive art. Each new generation of flower masters will continue to harness its artistic energies in developing new styles to meet the challenge of modern times, and to interpret the past through the eyes of the present.

VISIT TO AN EXHIBITION

A visit to an "all masters show" in Japan is an unforgettable experience. The spacious setting of such an exhibition is designed for dramatic impact. To emphasize the distinctive qualities of the different arrangements, displays are set in well-spaced niches against backgrounds of high-keyed colors.

Ikebana's long history is graphically portrayed by the country's leading flower masters. Each master exhibits his individual styles and school. Visitors would expect to find the flower masters using only natural materials related to flowers, but often all kinds of organic and inorganic materials are drawn together with surprising effectiveness. These modern masters have reached into other creative art forms and developed an avant-garde trend in sculpture, mobile, and relief which they incorporate into the realm of ikebana. Side by side with these modern creations appear the traditional styles of quiet, restrained beauty that echo the past.

Japan's love for flowers extends beyond the centers of learning and exhibition halls to the ordinary Japanese who invariably decorates his home, street stall, shop, and even a taxi with a single blossom or flowering spray. It is refreshing to find a modest arrangement in a waiting room of a busy railroad station and in other public places where one least expects to see flowers. It is not unusual to find spectacular modern designs in show windows of department stores, in theaters, hotel lobbies, and offices. In the cultural city of Kyoto one has the unexpected delight of finding cut flowers and foliage in a traffic policeman's booth in the middle of a busy intersection!

DIFFERENT FLORAL STYLES OF IKEBANA

Long before ikebana reached the masses and became a profession of flower masters, it was the leisurely pastime of Buddhist monks. The arranging of flowers was also regarded as an aristocratic accomplishment among the coterie of nobles and feudal lords. Prior to the fifteenth century no specific difference was drawn between flower arrangements of a religious nature and those for decorative use. It was during the reign of the eighth shogun, Yoshimasa Ashikaga (1435–1490) that the cultural arts of Japan became formalized. The shogun, a great patron of the arts, built the famed Silver Pavilion in Kyoto. It is now a museum, and regarded as the cradle of Japanese culture.

The following brief summary explains the varied floral styles, from the first formalized style established in the fifteenth century to the contemporary modern.

Rikka (RHI-kah—"standing flowers") was the earliest formalized style. It was originated by flower masters of the Ikenobo-ryu (RHI-yu—"school"), the oldest in Japan. Rikka was inspired by Chinese landscape paintings depicting symbolic mountains, hills, valleys, and streams. This large and elaborate style, in handsome bronze containers, decorated the palaces and temples of Japan's past. Specialized skill is required to execute the difficult Rikka. It follows strict adherence to prescribed formulas, and is divided into three forms: (*Shin*) Formal, (*Gyo*) Semiformal, and (*So*) Informal. Even though Rikka has been modified to keep step with the present, it remains extremely complicated, and a challenge to the flower arranger's skill. Rikka is seldom seen outside exhibition halls. It is taught only by the Ikenobo-ryu. The present *iemoto* (ee-EH-moh-toh—"headmaster") of this school is a young Buddhist monk—the forty-fifth descendant of the Ikenobo line of flower masters, dating back to Shotoku Taishi in the early seventh century.

14

Nageire or *Heika* (nah-GEH-ih-reh or HEY-kah, means "thrown in" and can be translated freely as "vase flowers"). These terms are synonymous, being different readings of the same Japanese ideographs. Some schools refer to this style as Nageire, others as Heika. It has been popular in Japan for centuries. Originally the term Nageire meant "any type of arrangement excepting Rikka." In later years it came to mean a free and unstudied way of arranging flowers and branches in a vase. Nageire took the place of the large and elaborate Rikka, which was not suitable for home decoration.

An extremely simple style was developed for the tea ceremony, using one or two flowers in a vase for the *tokonoma* (toh-koh-no-ma—"place of honor"), in the tea room. It was known as Chabana (cha-bah-nah) or "tea flowers."

Shoka or *Seika* (SHOH-kah or SAY-kah—different readings of the same ideographs, which can be translated as "living flowers"). Some schools refer to this style as Shoka, others as Seika.

Seika evolved from both the Rikka and Nageire styles. It has the elegance and rich symbolism of Rikka with the simplicity of Nageire. The Ikenobo flower masters applied Rikka's three forms of Formal, Semiformal, and Informal to the well-defined asymmetric triangle which became the framework for the Seika style. The restrained simplicity of this style made it suitable for the Japanese home. As the popularity of Seika spread beyond the elite circles to the masses, new schools made their appearance, each with its version of the symbolic triad. Those schools which prospered in the eighteenth century, and are still in existence, were Enshu-ryu, Ko-ryu, Kodo-ryu, and Misho-ryu. They are all offsprings of the Ikenobo-ryu.

Moribana (moh-RHI-bah-nah—"piled up flowers"). This extremely diversified style dates back to the late nineteenth century when Western influence swept Japan after its long seclusion from the world (1639–1858). Moribana was originated by Unshin Ohara, then an Ikenobo flower master. He founded his own school, the now prominent Ohara-ryu. Houn Ohara, grandson of the founder, is the present headmaster.

Moribana was a fresh departure from the stringent rules which governed the classical Rikka and Seika. While flowers and branches were still arranged within the symbolic triad, the scope of creativity was greatly increased. Plants of Western cultivation were introduced. Shallow containers of different shapes and textures were designed, and stimulated further interest in this new style. Moribana grew in popularity while the other styles waned.

The styles of Rikka, Seika, Nageire, and Moribana have all been modified with the changing times. Each school still retains its traditional form as well as a modern counterpart.

Free Style and *Avant Garde*.* Fresh vitality and inventiveness are evident in these modern forms which have broken away from closely bound rules of past centuries. Modern ikebana has brought about a change in artistic methods. The flower master who sparked the interest in this new movement is Sofu Teshigahara. He founded the Sogetsu School in 1926. Today, it is one of the largest flower schools in Japan. The free style and avant garde are extremely popular and are taught by many Japanese schools; however, some are more progressive than others.

Apart from the widely popular schools already mentioned (the three largest being Ikenobo, Ohara, and Sogetsu) there are other active schools too numerous to list. Among them are Saga-ryu, Ichiyo-ryu, Kofu-ryu, Shogen-ryu, Shofu-ryu, Seki-So-ryu, Kazan-ryu, and Wafu-kai-ryu.

* Free Style (*jiyu-bana*—gee-YU-bah-nah) and Avant Garde (*zen'ei bana*—zen-a-bah-nah) are better known by their Western terminology.

2   Elementary Design Principles

THE ART OF IKEBANA is so vast that no individual can master completely all the styles and the variations taught by the different schools. A set of fourteen rhythmic diagrams has, therefore, been worked out to give you, in broad principles, the fundamental patterns upon which the popular styles are based. These diagrams are not meant to be copied slavishly, but rather to train your eye in developing a sense of balance, proportion, and spatial relationships. Study them, practice them, then deviate from them. Subtle modifications can be created by changing the directional paths of a rhythmic pattern or simply by reversing the pattern. Examples of such variations are shown in the arrangements which accompany each diagram, except the classical style shown in figures 13a and 14a.

For practical application the radical lines are identified here as Principal, Secondary, and Tertiary. They are given distinctive markings. Principal, the tallest line, is indicated by a circle; the Secondary, by a square; and the Tertiary, by a triangle. All additional lines are attributes to one of the three radical lines.

In studying the diagrams you will notice that a triangle within a triangle weaves in and out of the framework of each design. For example, in Figure 1a, the radical lines form the framework of a distinct triangle. The attributes are composed of a smaller triangle. Still another triangle is formed by the Principal and Secondary lines and the attribute between them. Similarly, the Principal and Tertiary lines and the attributes between them form another triangle.

Flower arrangement, like other creative arts, cannot be confined to established formulas. The exact proportion of lines in a design, or the degree of slant in the lines and their directional paths change according to the materials and container used, as well as the environment in which the arrangement is placed. However, the measurements given in the diagrams for the radical lines and their visual relationships to the attributes will prove helpful in defining proportionate height, balance, rhythm, and depth.

Since the Principal line governs the over-all perspective

17

of a design, a guide is given in Figure 15 for its basic comparative height with different types of containers. The measurement for the Secondary line is three-fourths of the Principal, and the Tertiary line is three-fourths of the Secondary.

Japanese flower arrangements have three dimensions: height, breadth, and depth. Lines in a design do not point directly front, back, to the left or right, but are forward or backward *toward* the left or right. Different terms are used in the diagrams to describe the direction of lines—their height, breadth, and depth. They are upright, slightly forward (or backward), slanting forward (or backward), and leaning forward (or backward). In terms of degrees* they are as follows:

Upright line	90° perpendicular to 85°
Slightly forward (or backward)	85° to 50°
Slanting forward (or backward)	50° to 25°
Leaning forward (or backward)	25° to horizontal

* Some Japanese schools teach the degrees of angles in reverse, i.e., the perpendicular line is marked as 0° and the horizontal as 90°. In this book the fundamental geometric theory is used.

Exact placement of each line will depend on the nature of the branches and flowers used. The eye is generally the best judge to resolve the directional paths of lines within the variation of degrees (see figures 16 and 17).

Once the framework is balanced proportionately, the comparative heights of the attributes can easily be determined. They are shorter than each of their main lines. The attributes are used sparingly, and should interrelate harmoniously with the lines throughout the design.

In the simple diagram of Figure 1a lines of the framework move in advancing and receding paths to create fluid movement. Observe how the eye escapes confinement. It travels in and around the spaces of changing rhythmic balance. The Principal line is upright with a slight curve. The Secondary line, toward left, is slightly backward, and the Tertiary line, toward right, is slightly forward. Thus height, breadth, and depth are achieved with three radical lines. The attributes, used with restraint, are knit together with the framework in unifying relationships.

Knowledge of spatial and rhythmic harmony in design will come with practice. By charting your own expressive ideas based on the model diagrams, you will develop distinction and originality in your arrangements.

DESIGNS IN SHALLOW CONTAINERS (Moribana Style)

Moribana is an interpretive and widely popular style. Its different design classifications in shallow containers may be divided into Upright, Slanting, Horizontal, and Cascade. Naturalistic landscapes, water scenes, centerpieces, and studies emphasizing individual expression are all part of this imaginative style.

UPRIGHT DESIGNS

Figure 1a emphasizes tall-stemmed flowers with long, sturdy leaves. Flower suggestions: anthurium, belladonna lily, lily-of-the-Nile, gladiolus, iris, bird-of-paradise flower, torch lily, or ginger with their leaves, or with complementary foliage. (See Appendix listing synonyms and scientific names.)

The arrangement in Figure 1b is a slight variation of Figure 1a. Because of the natural curves in the foliage used, the design is placed to the right of container to maintain good balancing movements and spatial illusion.

Figure 2a emphasizes leafy branches for the framework, combined with short-stemmed flowers and foliage. Suggestions for the framework: loquat, rhododendron, Oregon grape, maple, heavenly bamboo, or pine. Suggestions for the flowers: pompom chrysanthemum, zinnia, aster, Barberton daisy (gerberia), camellia, windflower (anemone), daylily, or calla lily. Use either the leaves or flowers, or complementary foliage.

As will be the case in many illustrations, this design is reversed in order to show the variations possible from the basic pattern.

VERTICAL DESIGNS

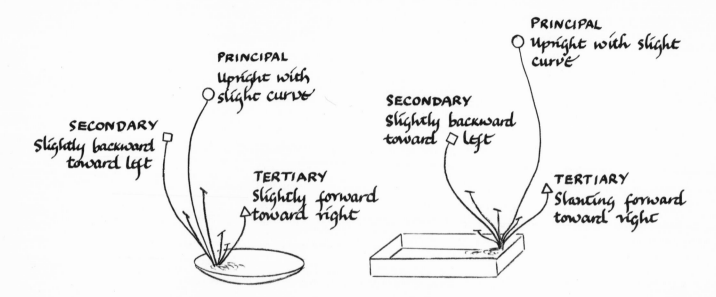

PRINCIPAL
Upright with slight curve

SECONDARY
Slightly backward toward left

TERTIARY
Slightly forward toward right

PRINCIPAL
Upright with slight curve

SECONDARY
Slightly backward toward left

TERTIARY
Slanting forward toward right

Figure 1a
PRINCIPAL: $1\frac{1}{2}$ × diameter of medium container
SECONDARY: $\frac{3}{4}$ of PRINCIPAL
TERTIARY: $\frac{1}{2}$ of SECONDARY ··

Figure 2a
PRINCIPAL: $1\frac{1}{2}$ × length of medium container
SECONDARY: $\frac{1}{2}$ of PRINCIPAL
TERTIARY: $\frac{1}{2}$ of SECONDARY

FIGURE 1b. The dramatic quality of deep red anthuriums is brought out in this simple study with bird's-nest ferns. Small rocks, adding a note of accent, conceal the holder in the speckled black-grey pottery bowl.

FIGURE 2b. Two loquat branches sketch the outline of this design, and five miniature calla lilies with their foliage nestle low in the center. Container is crackled grey porcelain.

21

The natural curves found in evergreens, flowering trees, or shrubs are ideal for figures 3a and 4a. Some examples are pine, juniper, fir, magnolia, Oregon grape, camellia, andromeda, azalea. Suggestions given for the flowers in Figure 2a can be used for these slanting designs. The combinations, however, are infinite.

Figure 3b illustrates an example of a branch used to symbolize a tree. The gnarled pine gives dramatic emphasis and becomes an expressive part of the design. Its lines spread over the open surface of the water, with low-growing flowers at its foot.

Drooping branches like weeping willow, weeping birch, or weeping mulberry are also effective. Use an oval- or rectangular-shaped container large enough to reflect the feeling of spatial illusion so important in this type of design.

Floral materials of a supple nature like pussy willow, broom, aspidistra, or dracaena will adapt well to the flowing lines of Figure 4a. Figure 4b shows the sparing use of leafy maple branches that have been carefully pruned to bring out their rhythmic qualities.

SLANTING DESIGNS

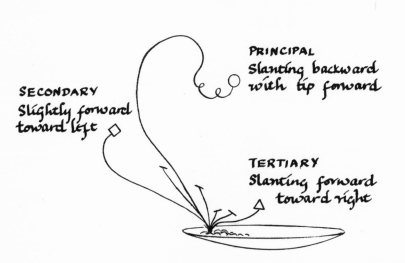

PRINCIPAL
Slanting backward
with tip forward

SECONDARY
Slightly forward
toward left

TERTIARY
Slanting forward
toward right

PRINCIPAL
Slanting backward
toward right

SECONDARY
Slightly forward
toward left

TERTIARY
Slanting forward
toward right

Figure 3a
PRINCIPAL: Twice length of
     medium container
SECONDARY: $\frac{1}{2}$ of PRINCIPAL
TERTIARY: $\frac{1}{3}$ of SECONDARY

Figure 4a
PRINCIPAL: $1\frac{1}{2}$ × length of
     medium container
SECONDARY: $\frac{1}{2}$ of PRINCIPAL
TERTIARY: $\frac{3}{4}$ of SECONDARY

24

FIGURE 3b. Distance lends enchantment to this woodland scene of a gnarled pine sweeping across the earthenware container. Small clusters of ribbon grass and daisies appear to be growing amid the rocks.

FIGURE 4b. Leafy maple branches spread their lines in a dark brown pottery container, and merge at the base with low-growing miniature chrysanthemums, ribbon grass, and sprays of maple. Small barks, covered with patina, artfully conceal the mechanics.

TABLE ARRANGEMENTS

When planning a centerpiece many underlying factors are taken into consideration—the size and type of table, its position in the room, and how the design is used. A centerpiece for a table appointment must be in absolute harmony with the varying textures and colors of the dinnerware, silver, glasses, and table linen. If the centerpiece is to be viewed from all sides, it should be below eye level. When a table is placed against a wall in a buffet setting, the design is seen from only three sides and its height need not be restricted. A centerpiece for a low coffee table may be either vertical or horizontal, but with an all-round perspective.

HORIZONTAL DESIGNS

The whirling lines of Figure 5a have varied possibilities. Branches, foliage, or flowers may be used for the framework. The design can be large and striking, or small and charming. In Figure 5b pine is the framework, with cyclamen and their foliage arranged low in the center. To compose a smaller arrangement, reduce the lines of the framework and size of container. The cyclamen grouping can be quite charming by itself. Other suggestions for flowers with their foliage are: gloxinia, Barberton daisy, or tulip. Leafy stemmed flowers like rose,

chrysanthemum, or peony are also suitable for this centerpiece design.

For a dramatic composition use anthurium, bird-of-paradise flower, torch lily, or gladiolus, and combine with leaves of the blossoms or strong textural foliage. Place the arrangement in a large container, and cover the mechanics with low foliage or driftwood.

A small receptacle will serve as a water holder when no container is used. It can be concealed by a low spread of foliage, or by a piece of weathered wood, as in Figure 52.

The practical and appealing design of Figure 6a can be composed with two flowers in a group and a third apart, or a cluster of three blossoms to one side of the container. Brandy bottle, water lily, lotus, and other water-growing plants, grouped low with their foliage, create a refreshing miniature pond scene. Large blossoms of peony, dahlia, hibiscus, cactus orchid, or tuberous begonia are most pleasing in a casual floating composition. Long sprays of foliage or vine may be added in a horizontal spread leading from the flowers. This design is also applied to compositions made with fruit or vegetables, known as *Morimono* (moh-RHI-moh-noh), arranged on a flat tray-shaped receptacle, or in a shallow basket.

Figure 6b shows a design with two flowers grouped together, and a third apart.

There are different ways of using the double horizontal grouping in Figure 7a, which may be arranged in small twin containers, as in Figure 7b, in one medium and one small container; or in a single large container. When two containers are used their shape, texture, and color should be either the same or harmoniously related. The groupings must also interrelate in the design, as in the camellia composition.

If a large, long container is used, the groupings should be well spaced, i.e., the left grouping should be in the far left, and the right grouping in the far right of the container. In a large round or square container, the groupings would be diagonally opposite each other. Design 14 (see Part II, below) is an example of this principle.

Flowering branches, blossoms, and foliage may be used by themselves or combined for these different designs. Suggestions are: azalea, camellia, soulangeana magnolia, rose, chrysanthemum, windflower (anemone), daisy, begonia or geranium.

Tall, graceful plants like the iris, lotus, or narcissus, grouped with their own leaves, are effective for Figure 8a. Slender grasses and reeds combined with water-growing plants make equally pleasing compositions. Figure 8b illustrates a large, oval container with Japanese irises. For other ideas use twin containers as in Figure 43, or combine a medium with a small container.

HORIZONTAL DESIGNS

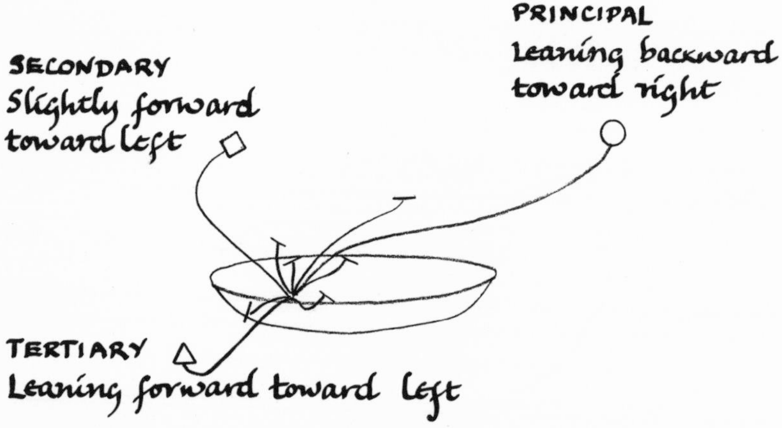

PRINCIPAL
Leaning backward
toward right

SECONDARY
Slightly forward
toward left

TERTIARY
Leaning forward toward left

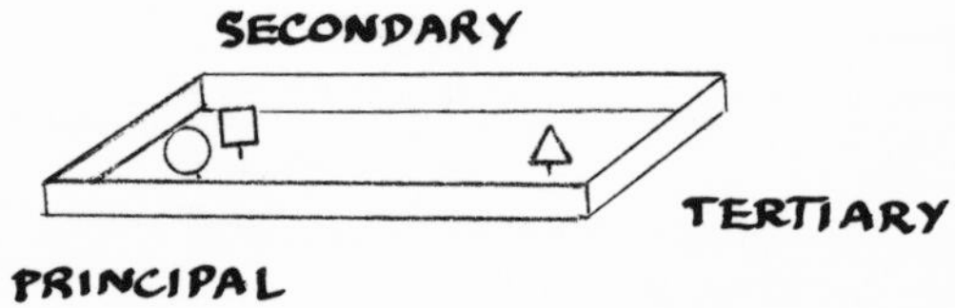

SECONDARY

PRINCIPAL

TERTIARY

Figure 5a
PRINCIPAL: 1½ x diameter of
            medium container
SECONDARY: ¾ of PRINCIPAL
TERTIARY: ¾ of SECONDARY

Figure 6a
No measurements. Stems are cut
very short for a floating effect.

FIGURE 5b.   Pine branches create the framework for this centerpiece with deep red cyclamen, their foliage overlapping one another. The smooth black lacquer bowl is chosen to complement the color and textural harmony of the floral materials.

FIGURE 6b.   Pale pink water lilies, in varying stages of development, appear to float among their pads. Open flowers suggest the present, while the bud and furled pad hold the promise of the future. This cool and refreshing arrangement is in a pale, seagreen porcelain bowl.

29

HORIZONTAL AND UPRIGHT DESIGNS
DOUBLE COMPOSITIONS

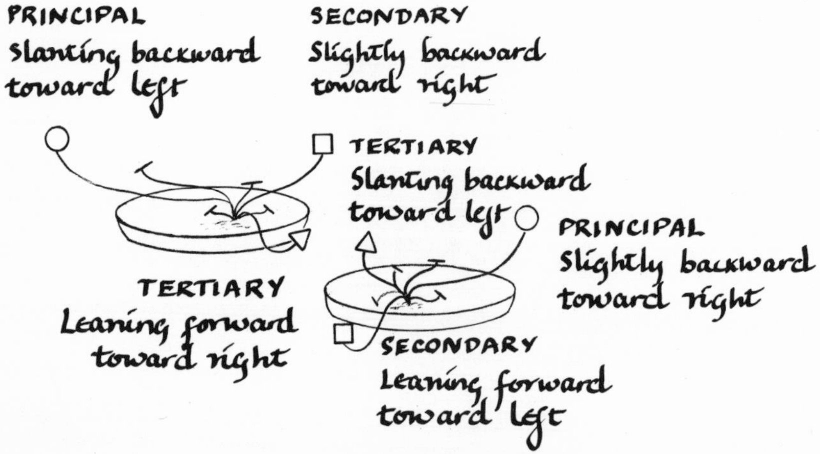

PRINCIPAL
Slanting backward
toward left

SECONDARY
Slightly backward
toward right

TERTIARY
Slanting backward
toward left

PRINCIPAL
Slightly backward
toward right

TERTIARY
Leaning forward
toward right

SECONDARY
Leaning forward
toward left

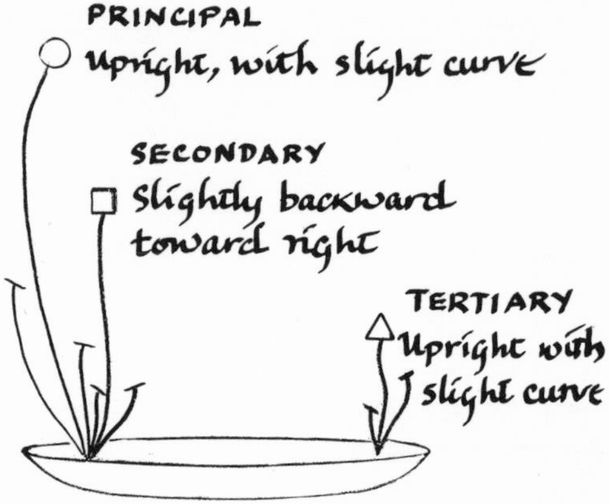

PRINCIPAL
Upright, with slight curve

SECONDARY
Slightly backward
toward right

TERTIARY
Upright with
slight curve

Figure 7a

PRINCIPAL: $1\frac{1}{4}$ × diameter of
small container

SECONDARY: $\frac{3}{4}$ of PRINCIPAL

TERTIARY: $\frac{3}{4}$ of SECONDARY

} Left Group

PRINCIPAL: Diameter of small
container

SECONDARY: $\frac{3}{4}$ of PRINCIPAL

TERTIARY: $\frac{3}{4}$ of SECONDARY

} Right Group

Figure 8a

PRINCIPAL: Length of large
container

SECONDARY: $\frac{3}{4}$ of PRINCIPAL

TERTIARY: $\frac{3}{4}$ of SECONDARY

30

FIGURE 7b. Delicate white camellias and their strong textural leaves make an appealing centerpiece in identical bowls of red lacquer.

FIGURE 8b. The slender, graceful Japanese iris with its strap blades is regarded as a water plant, and is frequently depicted in a spacious pool atmosphere. The grouping is called "fish path": Symbolic fish swim amid the cool shade of the leaves. Pebbles drifting in the ivory porcelain container create a feeling of serenity.

31

The sinuous curves of vines and shrubs are ideal for cascade designs since they will assume different rhythmic forms without destroying their own character and naturalness (Figure 9a). They are most pleasing when their trailing lines sweep downward. Some suggestions are: corkscrew willow, weeping willow, snow willow, bridal wreath, wisteria, morning glory, passion flower vine, woodbine, or greenbrier. If flowers are added, they should be used sparingly to maintain an airy composition.

The cascade Moribana is seen to best advantage when placed on a wall shelf or on a tall pedestal. Figure 9b illustrates an arrangement on a pedestal; and Figure 54, in Chapter 6, an arrangement on a floating wall shelf.

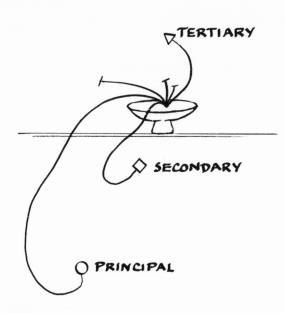

TERTIARY

SECONDARY

◇

○ PRINCIPAL

Figure 9a

Note: Since the cascade design varies considerably with the different kinds of floral materials used, no standard measurements or angle of placement can be given. The eye is the best judge.

FIGURE 9b. Two red tulips with their foliage are centered between the sinuous lines of corkscrew willow arranged in a white porcelain container. The tall white marble pedestal gives height and textural contrast to the design.

33

VASE DESIGNS (Nageire Style)

The Nageire style has three forms: Upright, Slanting, and Cascade. Arrangements in a vase are generally more pleasing when placed on a fairly low surface. In a cascade design, however, the lines become more dramatic when the container is suspended above eye level, and silhouetted against a plain wall, as in Figure 12a.

Floral materials vary according to the shape and texture of the container used. The narrow vase in Figure 10a harmonizes with slender or wispy branches and flowers, whereas the wide vase in Figure 11a is compatible with similar strong textures of branches and flowers.

The cascade form of Nageire may be applied to either a tall vase or a hanging type. Floral materials with flowing lines will provide vivacity for the vase or hanging design.

Suggestions given for floral materials in Figure 9b are also applicable to vase designs. Materials of sturdy nature that combine well in a wide, strong-textured vase are magnolia, camellia, rhododendron, plum, peach, cherry, lilac, maple, pine, or juniper.

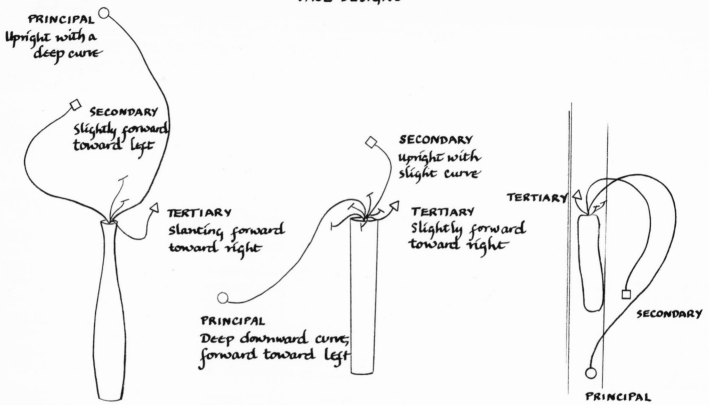

PRINCIPAL
Upright with a
deep curve

SECONDARY
Slightly forward
toward left

TERTIARY
Slanting forward
toward right

SECONDARY
Upright with
slight curve

TERTIARY
Slightly forward
toward right

PRINCIPAL
Deep downward curve,
forward toward left

TERTIARY

SECONDARY

PRINCIPAL

UPRIGHT

Figure 10a
PRINCIPAL: 1½ x height of medium vase
SECONDARY: ¼ of PRINCIPAL
TERTIARY: ½ of SECONDARY

SLANTING

Figure 11a
PRINCIPAL: 1½ x height of medium vase
SECONDARY: ½ of PRINCIPAL
TERTIARY: ⅓ of SECONDARY

Figure 12a
See reference note
under Figure 9a

36

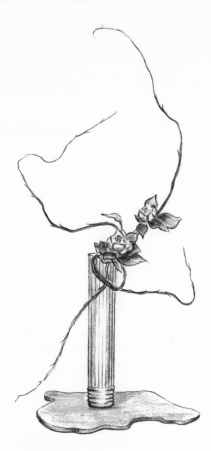

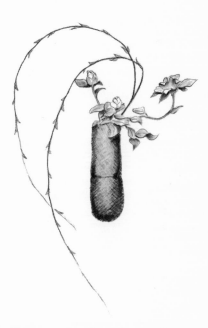

Figure 10b. The balancing lines of wisteria tendrils encircle pink camellias nestled in their sturdy leaves. The tall narrow container, set on a burl base, is made of dark wood slats.

Figure 11b. The stark simplicity of a white magnolia and its green-brown foliage interrelate in texture and color harmony with the tawny tones of the modern pottery vase.

Figure 12b. Fragrant small gardenias and their thick leaves are spread in a hanging bamboo basket to balance the wispy, drooping lines of weeping willow.

Unlike the other floral styles, Seika is governed by inflexible rules, measurements, and directional paths. Although the different classical schools teach their own versions of this style, there is nevertheless strong stylistic likeness in the linear perspective. Only the trained eye is able to distinguish one school from another.

Of the three basic forms in the Seika style—(*Shin*) Formal, (*Gyo*) Semiformal, and (*So*) Informal—only the Formal Seika is given because of its adaptability to diverse floral materials. The other two forms are variations of the Formal. Figures 13a and 14a are diagrams of the Koryu School. They are the right-hand and left-hand forms of the Formal Seika.

You will notice that the Principal line is shaped like an archer's bow. It rises directly above the center of the container, with the tip and base in perfect alignment. The Secondary and Tertiary lines merge with the base of the Principal, about 3 to 4 inches above the water line, to a point of diversion on either side of the Principal. This union of stems represents a symbolic idea of a plant growing from the surface of the soil.

The length of the Principal is based on visual appeal and its relationship to the container. This line may vary from one and one-half to six times the diameter of a shallow container, or height of a tall container. Once the length of the Principal line is established, the Secondary and Tertiary lines are always one-half and one-third of the Principal, when curved.

The directional path for the Secondary line slants forward, and the Tertiary line slants backward. The concave or hollow side of the Principal always faces the concave side of the Tertiary. The number of "attributes" that are supplementary to the framework depends on the type of material and container selected. It is important that each "attribute" be placed in such a manner that it appears as part of the structural outline. All lines point their tips toward the Principal. In the diagrams four "attributes" are given: two for the Principal, one for the Secondary, and one for the Tertiary.

The three radical lines may be composed of strong, firm evergreens, flowering branches, foliage, or flowers with foliage. One of the most satisfying effects is the purity of line achieved in a classical study. The base of stems in a shallow container is concealed by small pebbles banked on the holder, or by a rock. Short foliage is never used at the base. This will destroy the rhythm of the design.

Despite the restriction of artistic freedom in the classical style, there is, nevertheless, spatial tension in a three-dimensional design, with extraordinarily expressive lines. Study of this style will prove most helpful in understanding the faultless balance, rhythm, and depth which exist in all Japanese designs.

CLASSICAL DESIGNS
(Seika Style)

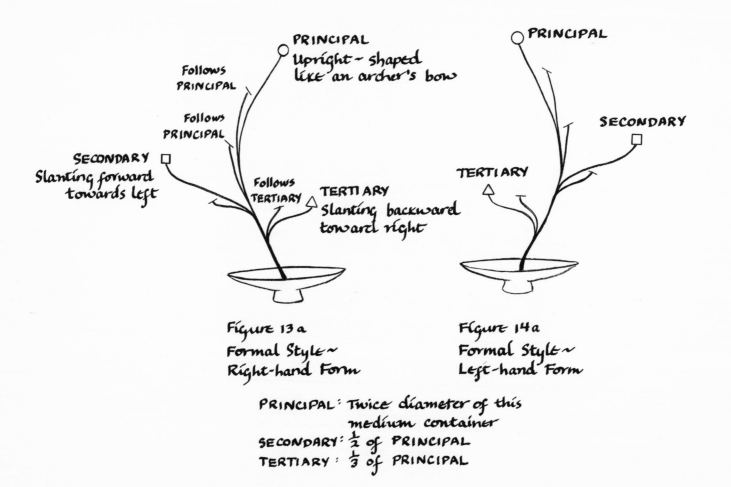

PRINCIPAL Upright ~ shaped like an archer's bow

Follows PRINCIPAL

Follows PRINCIPAL

SECONDARY Slanting forward towards left

Follows TERTIARY

TERTIARY Slanting backward toward right

PRINCIPAL

SECONDARY

TERTIARY

Figure 13 a
Formal Style ~
Right-hand Form

Figure 14a
Formal Style ~
Left-hand Form

PRINCIPAL: Twice diameter of this
medium container
SECONDARY: $\frac{1}{2}$ of PRINCIPAL
TERTIARY: $\frac{1}{3}$ of PRINCIPAL

FIGURE 13b. Three pink roses, in different degrees of development, emerge gracefully from a white porcelain bowl. The "attributes" are two short leafy rose stems added to the Principal and Tertiary lines to provide depth. Tiny pebbles bank the holder.

FIGURE 14b. Five pussy willows, perfectly balanced, appear to be growing out of the bronze sampan set on dark brown bamboo slats. The taller "attribute" is placed close to the left of the Principal; the shorter one, to the right of the Tertiary. Tiny pebbles cover the holder and drift into the expanse of water.

41

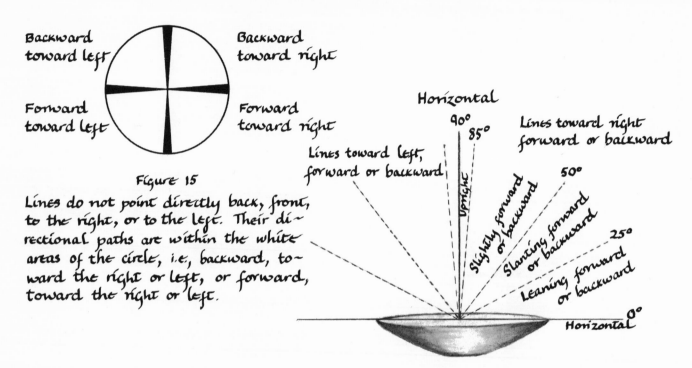

Figure 15

Lines do not point directly back, front, to the right, or to the left. Their directional paths are within the white areas of the circle, i.e., backward, toward the right or left, or forward, toward the right or left.

Figure 16

Upright	90° ~ 85°
Slightly forward (or backward) toward right or left	85° ~ 50°
Slanting forward (or backward) toward right or left	50° ~ 25°
Leaning forward (or backward) toward right or left	25° ~ 0°

BASIC MEASUREMENT FOR PRINCIPAL LINE
WITH COMPARABLE CONTAINER
(part of height is absorbed by container and curve of line)

SHALLOW CONTAINERS

Diameter + depth : Small

1½ × diameter + depth : Medium

Twice diameter + depth : Large

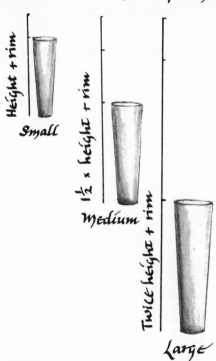

Vase
Small: 10" - 12"
Medium 12" - 17"
Large: 17" - 20"

Figure 17   The measurement of diameter + depth refers to round or square containers. For oval or rectangle containers, measurement is based on length + depth.

Small: round or square	8" - 10"
Medium: " " "	10" - 12"
Large: " " "	12" - 16"
Small: oval or rectangle	10" - 12"
Medium: " " "	12" - 16"
Large: " " "	16" - 20"

43

3   Basic Techniques

W E CAN LEARN from the Japanese how to develop faultless balance and proper plant grooming in an arrangement. By following these illustrated techniques, flower arranging will become infinitely easier. Using the right mechanical aids, knowing how to trim a leafy branch, bend a straight stem, or grade and furl leaves—all contribute to the final appearance of a well-planned arrangement. The supports which balance flowers and branches in a tall vase or shallow container vary according to the size and shape of receptacle, as well as the floral materials used.

SHALLOW CONTAINER SUPPORTS

Needle-point holders with a heavy metal base are the best supports in shallow containers. Normally this type of holder will support virtually any floral material. There are, however, specific techniques for the exceptions, which are also illustrated.

To secure a thick branch in a holder, cut it at a slant on the side opposite the direction in which it will lean. First insert the branch upright, then incline it to the desired angle with the tip forced securely into the holder (Figure 18).

When heavy branches require additional support, place another needle-point holder, face down, on the edge of the one being used. This counterbalances the weight. Mechanics can be concealed either by foliage, weathered wood, or rocks (Figure 19).

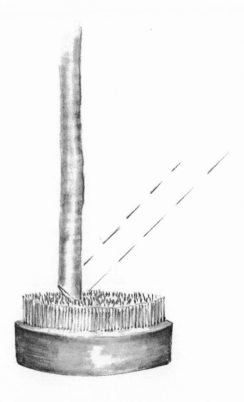

FIGURE 18

FIGURE 19

To retain the balance of a soft, hollow stem, insert a slender woody branch, about 1½ inches long, within the stem (Figure 20).

A thin or soft stem can be made firmer in the holder by tying it to a slender woody twig. This technique is also applied to a flower or branch that is too short for the arrangement. Be sure to submerge the joined part in sufficiently deep water (Figure 21).

FIGURE 20

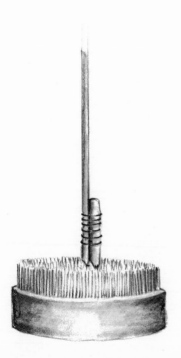

FIGURE 21

VASE SUPPORTS

An excellent support for a narrow, tall vase is made with a long sturdy **Y**-shaped branch. Length of support should be about 1 inch below the rim of vase. Split tip of branch about 1½ inches to support wispy materials, and a deeper cut for heavier branches or stems (Figure 22).

When thick branches or stems are arranged in a wide vase, a cross-support will give secure balance. This is made of two slender, sturdy branches cut to fit snugly across the container, and tied in the center with florist wire. A diagonal cut on the branch end will give additional support to materials that rest against walls of the vase (Figure 23).

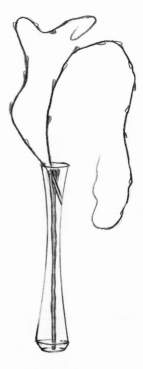

FIGURE 22

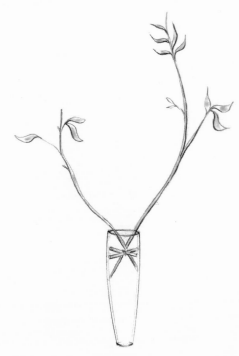

FIGURE 23

HOW TO BEND BRANCHES AND STEMS

Branches and stems, which seldom have the right curves for an arrangement, can be given more rhythmic appearance by bending their lines. To curve a flower stem, place hands between the leaves and bend gradually with a slight twisting motion to prevent the stem from snapping (Figure 24).

In bending a slender branch, place thumbs close together and apply gentle pressure until the curve takes shape (Figure 25).

A thick branch requires more pressure when forming a curve. Grasp branch with both hands, exerting force with the left thumb. Bend gradually, just short of breaking. Slight incisions made in different parts of the branch will induce it to bend, particularly if it is not flexible (Figure 26).

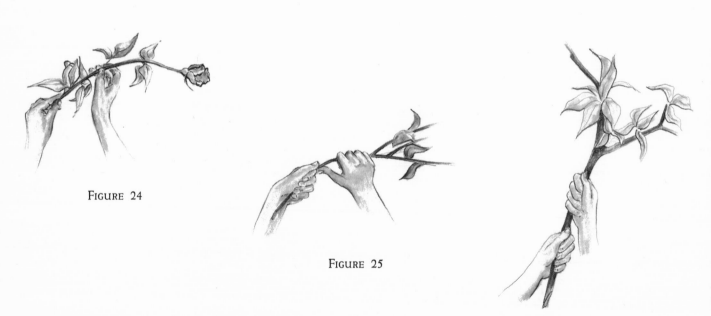

FIGURE 24

FIGURE 25

FIGURE 26

HOW TO TRIM AND FURL LEAVES

Wide, long leaves can be trimmed to appear narrow and shorter by gliding scissors along the margin of the leaf, following its contour to retain a natural appearance. This technique is extremely helpful when grading leaves for an arrangement. Figures 27 and 28 show a calla lily leaf before and after trimming.

FIGURE 27

FIGURE 28

49

A long tapered leaf can be furled by rolling the tip around a slender pencil or stick, as shown in Figure 29. For a tighter furl, roll the leaf between wet fingertips. Then place furled leaf between heels of the palms and roll briskly. Figure 30 illustrates the tight furl of an aspidistra leaf (cast iron plant); and Figure 31 a loose furl of striped dracaena.

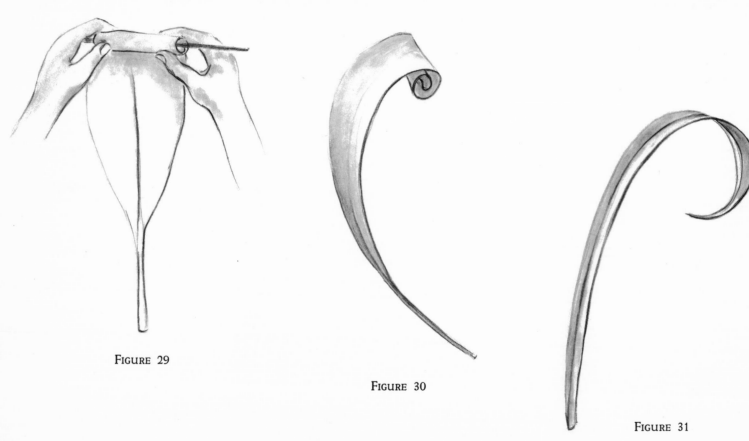

FIGURE 29

FIGURE 30

FIGURE 31

HOW TO GROUP AND WATER-JOIN
STRAP BLADES

The appearance of tall narrow blades often can be improved by separating them from the flower stem and then regrouping them to dramatize the natural characteristics of their growth.

Figure 32 shows two examples of regrouping the stiff gladiolus leaves to achieve flowing motion in a design.

Figure 33 illustrates three groupings of iris blades arranged in the natural manner of growth. Note that the tips of leaves point inward, and that each clump is composed of varying heights. These characteristics are frequently emphasized in natural iris studies.

The technique of grouping the leaves securely together is known as water-joining. This is done by gently rubbing the base of a leaf with a wet rag, and then pressing two or three leaves together to form a clump. Base of leaves should appear as a single growing unit.

FIGURE 32

FIGURE 33

HOW TO GROOM FLOWERS AND BRANCHES

A flower can take on a more graceful or dramatic appearance if its leaves are correctly pruned, and the stem is curved. In Figure 34 the natural state of the rose looks rigid and ungroomed. After trimming some of the leaves and bending the stem, the flower appears more graceful, as in Figure 35. Note how the natural distribution of leaves is still retained on either side of the stem. In trimming, bear in mind that the end result must give the appearance of clear-cut natural lines. This grooming technique is applied to the profuse growth of any type of foliage or blossoms.

FIGURE 34

FIGURE 35

One of the more difficult aspects of flower arrangement is to find the best rhythmic lines of a leafy branch, particularly when it is used for the framework. A word of caution—before reaching for a pair of scissors, study every line of the branch. Then prune.

Figures 37–39 show the results of careful trimming of the rhododendron branch in Figure 36. The lines *B* and *C* were severed from the main branch *A*. *C* was discarded. The lower leaves were removed from *A*, and the leafy tips thinned. The lower leaves of *B* were removed to emphasize the curve of the branch. These illustrations also show the adaptability of the two branches used for the same framework to three different containers.

FIGURE 36

FIGURE 37

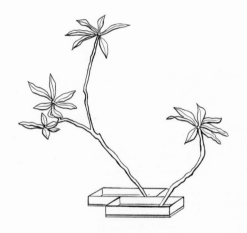

FIGURE 38

FIGURE 39

55

4   Care of Cut Flowers and Foliage

THE LIFE EXPECTANCY of cut floral materials can be prolonged by following a few simple practices. Cut greens and flowers from the florist, or your garden, should be immersed immediately in a deep container of water and left in a cool, dark place for a few hours. This conditioning process will prevent rapid moisture evaporation through the breathing cells of the plants. Spray the floral materials with cool water to increase the humidity in the atmosphere.

The best time for garden cuttings is just after sundown, when plants have built up a day-long supply of food, or before sunrise, while dew is still heavy on the petals and leaves. Flowers cut in an early stage of development will last longer than the more mature ones.

Floral materials should be cut with a sharp blade, either a knife or flower scissors. If the blade is not sharp it will mangle the stems. A slant cut will expose more of the plant cells and increase the absorption of water, since the slanting end does not rest flat in the container.

Cutting stems under water is a further aid to preserving plants, for it prevents air bubbles from entering the open cells of the moisture-conducting vessels. Air bubbles in plant cells impede the intake of water. When stems are cut under water they should not be taken out immediately and exposed to the air. This will defeat the purpose of cutting under water.

The condition of the water in the flower container is important. Before arranging your floral materials, allow the water to stand for a few minutes, permitting air to escape. Water-soluble chemicals, available at most florists, added to the water will lengthen the life span of cut plants. A small piece of charcoal in the container will act as a purifier, and also help to eliminate offensive odors of some plants. Rinse the charcoal in water before using it, so as to remove dust particles. If the charcoal is placed near the holder it will be concealed from view.

Branches and stems should be well submerged in water to prevent them from wilting rapidly. Add fresh water daily to the container, so that the water line will remain at the same level. Flowers and foliage will wither with unnecessary speed in an atmosphere that is too warm or dry. A daily mist bath will freshen the appearance and perk up wilted flowers or foliage (Figure 40).

FIGURE 40.   A daily mist bath with cool water will freshen the appearance of a flower arrangement and perk up wilted blossoms or leaves. This treatment also increases the humidity in a dry or warm atmosphere.

57

SPECIAL CONDITIONING TECHNIQUES

The Japanese make a practice of using different conditioning techniques to prolong the life of cut plants which do not respond to fresh water alone. Since plants vary in their lasting qualities, treatments differ.

Searing and hot water treatments are excellent for woody and bleeding plants. Some examples of woody branches and herbaceous woody stems are flowering quince, lilac, crabapple, perennial chrysanthemums, hydrangea, and wisteria. Bleeding plants are those which exude a milky, yellow, or colorless texture, like dahlia, hollyhock, poinsettia, poppy, and oleander. Generally, they respond better to searing than hot water.

For the searing treatment, split the branch or stem end about one inch, then hold above candle flame for several seconds. This treatment should be repeated each time the stem or branch end is recut. When applying the hot water treatment, immerse at least three inches of the stem or branch end in hot water. Allow to remain until water cools. Protect foliage and blossoms from rising steam with a covering of soft paper.

The Japanese use a special pump implement for injecting cool water (or a mild solution of strained tobacco) into stems of flowers and foliage of a honeycombed nature which do not draw up sufficient water after they have been cut. The liquid is forced slowly into the stem, gradually penetrating the blossoms and foliage.

Peppermint oil is extremely helpful in preserving a variety of cut plants. The stem or branch end should be dipped in the peppermint oil for just a few seconds, after it has been conditioned in water. Some of the flowering shrubs and blossoms which respond to this treatment are acacia, bougainvillea, hardy asters, California poppy, canna, Chinese agrimony, cosmos, gardenia, geranium, gerberia, gloxinia, honeysuckle, plantain lily, Japanese quince, jasmine, wisteria, and zinnia.

It should be stressed here that most cut plants will hold up amazingly well with the simple care mentioned earlier in this chapter; and with the aid of commercial chemical preparations the life span of plants will be prolonged.

5   Flower Containers and Basic Equipment

A MODEST STOCK of well-chosen containers is the starting point to successful flower arranging. The container is a vital part of the composition. It should enhance the flowers and foliage, and become a single harmonious whole. Containers of neutral colors will blend with the decor of most homes, and simple shapes will adapt to frequent use. A selection of basic shapes is shown in Figure 41.

The Japanese excel in their designs of imaginative flower containers. They make use of natural forms such as gourds, shells, rugged bark, wormwood, and rock. Natural containers are numerous and extremely varied if one is aware of these treasures. The flower arranger's bounty comes from the mountain, hillside, woods, and sea. Lava, soft rock, bark, gnarled or weathered wood make fascinating containers. A boat or bucket of seasoned wood is unique. Baskets are useful. A small container placed in the boat, bucket, or basket will serve as a water holder. While transparent crystal and glass are beautiful, they are not as practical as opaque containers which conceal mechanical aids.

You do not need the skill of an expert to make your own containers. With a little resourcefulness you can improvise, using jars, bowls, boxes, wine bottles, and baking pans. Some can be sprayed with enamel finish to resemble lacquer, or painted a flat pastel for a soft effect. Twine wrapped tightly around a wine bottle, jar, or baking pan makes a practical, rustic container. Plumber's lead, or soft copper, is flexible enough to be molded into any shape once it is cut to a specific size. Before applying a finish, clean the surface thoroughly with steel wool. Copper can be oxidized in a sulphur solution for an antique appearance. Figures 43–50 illustrate some improvised containers.

Use your ingenuity to make flower bases out of plastic, glass, tile, wood, or masonite. They can be cut professionally in varying shapes and sizes. Rugged flat weathered wood is another source for excellent bases because of the interesting contours and natural textures. A round, oval, square, or rectangular base can be cut in half and the two pieces used either staggered or together. If stained or lacquered a different color on either side a base becomes more versatile (see Figure 42).

BASIC EQUIPMENT

Correct tools are important. You will need a pair of sharp scissors, a small saw to cut heavy branches, and a sharp knife to scrape the ends of woody stems and branches. Any bottle with an atomizer will serve as a water sprayer to freshen cut floral materials after they have been arranged. Keep on hand a selection of differently shaped needle-point holders, sturdy branches to make vase supports, and florist wire. A few good rocks and tiny pebbles are valuable additions to enhance some of your floral studies. Collect interesting shapes of weathered wood to incorporate in an arrangement. Add to your kit a heavy waterproof sheet (oilcloth or plastic) to protect the finish of a table surface used as working area. Small felt pads or rubber tips on the bottom of

containers and bases will prevent scratches on polished surfaces.

Always keep your tools sharp, clean, and dry. From time to time immerse your "washable" flower containers in soapy water to rid them of any settled bacteria. Time and energy will be saved if the containers and all essential equipment are stored together in an accessible place.

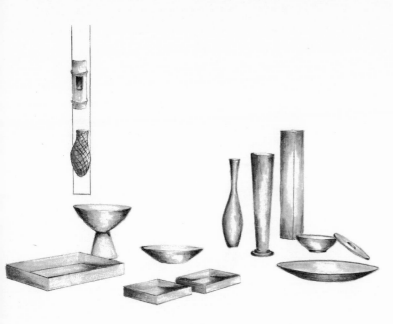

FIGURE 41. A modest selection of basic containers in neutral colors will adapt to frequent use.

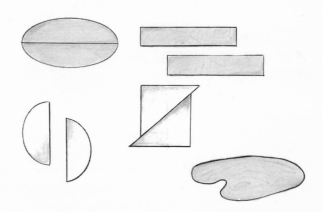

FIGURE 42. Varied shapes of flower bases.

61

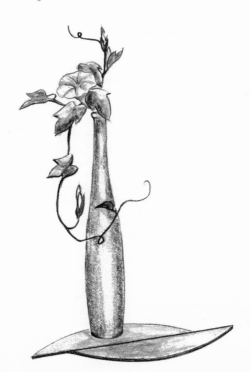

FIGURE 44. A tall, slender wine bottle of dark red serves as a useful vase for this casual arrangement of morning glories. The "half-moon" bases are plywood, lacquered black on one side and dark green on the other.

FIGURE 43. A two-tiered lacquer box of burnt orange is used as a double container. The lid, tilted on the rim of the front container, adds further charm to this natural study of paper-white narcissus. Water holders can be placed in various boxes or baskets to achieve a similar effect.

FIGURE 46. This square container is a baking pan well coated with jet black lacquer paint. It is most practical. Arrangement is composed of slender rhythmic spirea combined with calla lilies and their foliage.

FIGURE 45. A narrow, rugged plaque of weathered wood is used for the hanging arrangement of red geraniums. Container is an openwork basket. A glass jar, painted brown to blend in with the basket, holds water.

FIGURE 48. The rectangular redwood container, lined with oxidized copper, is adaptable to infinite designs. Fir branches and daylilies in the pictured arrangement appear to be growing amid rocks in a woodland scene.

Any well-made wood receptacle, with tight joints, can be waterproofed by heavy applications of sealing compound and clear lacquer.

FIGURE 47. The natural depression in the soft irregularly shaped rock is used to advantage. It is lined with oxidized copper. Streaked red and white belladonna lilies and their swordlike leaves lend a striking contrast to the rugged container.

Another useful, natural container can be made of weathered wood with a hollow opening. It does not have to be lined; a small can or jar placed in the hollow will be concealed from view.

64

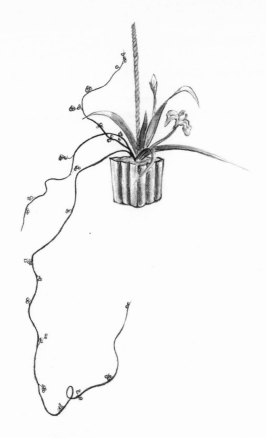

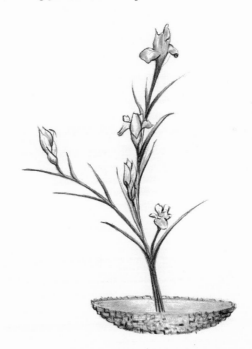

FIGURE 50. Dutch irises in a restrained classical study enhance this unique container. Tiny shells of beige and brown tones are cemented together to cover a round glass bowl. Inside of container is beige; a special plastic paint for glass was used. This self-setting paint does not chip.

FIGURE 49. The flowing lines of dried bittersweet combined with Japanese iris and their blades create an unusual study for this rustic bucket. It is made of split wood dowels nailed to thin plywood boards and coated with dark wood stain. A small can holds water. Rope hangs from a metal ring anchored in the center on a bar of wood. (If clear lacquer is sprayed on freshly picked bittersweet, the berries will not shrivel.)

6   Planning Your Floral Design

THE EXPRESSION AND spirit of a floral design are felt only in compatible surroundings. Study your environment. The setting is important. No matter how striking your design may be, it will appear confused and lost among unrelated ornaments and other objects. If you place the same design in a setting with a few well-chosen objects, suddenly its emotional elements evoke attention. Avoid areas that are overheated, drafty, or exposed to excessive sunlight. Floral materials cannot survive under these conditions.

One satisfactory way to achieve harmony, proportion, and balance is first to work out the design in the area where it will be placed. Put a heavy waterproof sheet over the surface area to prevent scratches and water stains. Experiment with different shapes of vases and bowls until you feel you have the right color, texture, and container shape in relation to the surroundings.

After you have decided on the container, consider the type of floral materials that will combine harmoniously with it. If the container is rustic, carry out similar strong textures in the floral materials, or if the container is smooth or delicate, use complementary flowers and foliage. Let the nature of the branches and flowers express themselves. Never force them into unnatural shapes. Keep your design as simple as possible. Use not more than two or three contrasting materials of branches, flowers, and foliage. Sketch the composition mentally and try to visualize it in its particular setting. This frequently helps when you are uncertain in the planning stage. To bring about dramatic expression in a design there should be a contrast of light and dark tones and textures merging in perfect coordination with the container and floral materials—all harmoniously attuned to the environment.

If you are following a specific design, do not attempt to make an exact copy of it, since no two branches or flowers grow alike. Use the model as a guide, but let your creative sense express the spirit and feeling you want to achieve. By challenging the imagination, your arrangement will reflect an intrinsic, personal quality.

The floral materials must be fresh. Select blossoms in the budding stage, so that you can enjoy their development as they gradually open up, and strong, sturdy branches and foliage. Remove all bruised, dense, or withered foliage and blossoms before placing the floral materials in a deep container of water close to your working area. This will simplify the final grooming. Keep your scissors, saw, knife, water sprayer, and other basic materials within easy reach. Fill the container with water. The holder in a shallow container must be large enough to accommodate all the materials without crowding them. To prevent the holder from sliding, place a soft piece of paper or a thin rubber mat under it. Now you are ready to begin arranging your floral materials. The form of the longest line determines the arrangement. For instance, if the curve of the line leans to the right, facing you, the arrangement should be placed toward the left end of the container to provide spatial balance. Keep the branch or stem ends close together in the holder, even though the upper part of the lines may spread out. Leave sufficient room for the flowers and foliage to be arranged within the outline. When the framework is completed, study the lines to see if they have good balancing movements. The framework should not give the impression that it is precariously balanced. Sometimes by changing the height or directional path of a line, continuity of rhythm can be achieved. Trimming superfluous lines may also make an astonishing difference. The flowers and foliage should integrate with the structural outline in a rhythmic and harmonious relationship. Each flower has its individual appeal. Some are more attractive when arranged in profile, while others show up better with their heads reaching upward.

Japanese arrangements are generally more pleasing when placed off-center in a container. There are, of course, exceptions, as in the classical style.

To carry out the spatial illusion, about one-third of the container is used. The rest of it shows clear water. In a vase, the open area is lightly covered by leaves which rise above and over the rim.

There are different ways of concealing the mechanics. Clusters of foliage may be arranged to appear as though they are growing naturally. An interesting piece of weathered wood makes an artistic camouflage. Rugged or water-worn rocks, which add realism to a woodland or pond scene in a shallow container, will help to cover the holder. Smooth pebbles may be used to bank the holder, with a few drifting into the open water to suggest movement of the current. All these finer points of detail give distinction to Japanese floral designs.

FINAL TOUCHES

After your arrangement is completed, the final touches of grooming will be necessary. Perhaps only a snip here and there is all that is needed to remove nonessentials that may clutter a design, such as drooping flowers or heavy clusters, and twigs or foliage on the underside of a branch. Remember that a good design has clean lines, depth, spatial illusion, and balancing movements. It should never have the appearance of a contrived effort.

Enjoy your arrangements longer by adding fresh blossoms or foliage to replace the wilted ones. If the structural line is composed of enduring branches and foliage it will keep for several weeks. Use the same outline in a different container for a change in the design, or rearrange the outline for an entirely different composition.

Daily care will prolong the life span of cut floral materials. Water in the container should be changed at least twice a week to remove any settled bacteria. A daily mist bath over the entire arrangement will restore loss of moisture evaporation, and give a continued fresh look to the flowers and foliage.

FIGURE 51. *Hall Setting* Tall lines of screw pine combined with low, clustered geraniums in a white porcelain bowl are in pleasing harmony with the white marble-top table. Note how the upward, reaching lines in the floral design are balanced by the oval hanging mirror in an uncluttered background. Magazines are placed casually on the table to give the impression of a natural rather than contrived setting.

FIGURE 52. *Centerpiece* Furled aspidistra leaves merged with a gnarled piece of weathered wood make a striking composition for the center of this teak table. An all-foliage design is practical because of its enduring quality.

FIGURE 53. *Vase Study for a Dining Room* The color harmony of this setting is in buff, brown, and orange tones. The slender vase of brown-speckled porcelain blends in with the mahogany chest. Dark spiny stems of Australian pine which wrap around the sunburst thistle of buff tones, are the dried materials for this modern design. In the background is an abstract painting of similar tonal shadings with splashes of orange, which are picked up by the same color of the antique lacquered bowls.

FIGURE 54. *Cascade Design for a Wall Shelf* Drooping lines of a weeping willow limb lean over a floating wall shelf. The slanting branch is balanced by upright lines of streaked orange-white belladonna lilies and their sturdy leaves. The earthenware container blends in with the shelf and brown leather book ends.

PART II

24 Basic Designs
with Step-by-Step Instructions

DESIGN 1

This natural composition of rising miscanthus grass merged with small yellow chrysanthemums in an oval earthenware bowl, expresses the mood of autumn.

Materials

1. 5 long stems of miscanthus grass
   Substitutes: cattail, scouring rush, or pampas grass
2. 5 small chrysanthemums
   Substitutes: aster, pompom dahlia, marigold, daisy, zinnia, or windflower (anemone)
3. 3"–4" needle-point holder
4. Oval or rectangular medium container

Method

Cut miscanthus grass in irregular heights. Trim long leaves to avoid clutter. Arrange stems in a natural upright manner with leaves giving the impression they are swaying in the wind. Steps 6, 7, and 9 form a triangle. Step 6 is slightly backward. Step 7 is leaning forward. Step 9 is slightly forward, toward left. Steps 8 and 10 give low depth to the arrangement. They lean forward toward the left and right. Add a few long wisps of foliage close to steps 8 and 10, with tips rising over the rim of container. Cover holder with short foliage of the flowers.

74

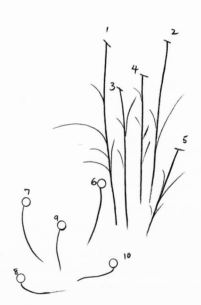

DESIGN 2

Tall, slender blades of ribbon grass rise freely above a low spread of orange browallia in a natural study. The blue porcelain container is in pleasing harmony with the floral materials.

Materials
1. 5 tall, narrow blades of ribbon grass
   Substitutes: Cane reeds, feather grass, pampas grass, or miscanthus
2. 4 leafy stems of browallia
   Substitutes: Acacia, sweet alyssum, begonia, or bouvardia
3. 3"–4" needle-point holder
4. Medium container with stem base

Method
Cut blades in irregular heights. Arrange them upright and close together with their tips spreading out. (Diagram shows two natural clusters of leaves.) The leafy stems of browallia are also cut in varying heights. Step 3, the longest line, is slightly forward. Step 4 is slightly backward. Step 5 is slightly forward, toward right, and Step 6 is leaning forward, toward left, with some flowers brushing lightly over rim of container. Cover holder with additional leaves.

77

DESIGN 3

A solitary, deep-red Barberton daisy rises above its own rich foliage in a design of restrained simplicity. Container is pale green porcelain.

Materials

1. 1 tall Barberton daisy (gerberia)
    Substitutes: Use a flower with bare stem—anthurium, bird-of-paradise flower, calla lily, torch lily, or plantain lily
2. 3 leaves of flower used
3. 3″–4″ needle-point holder
4. Florist wire; short woody stem
5. Medium container with stem base

Method

To prevent the long stem from either turning or falling due to its own weight, tie it to a short woody stem for secure support in the holder. Insert flower stem in the holder upright, and then incline it slightly backward. Cut leaves in varying heights. Step 2 is leaning forward, with leaf brushing lightly over rim of container. Step 3 is slightly backward. Step 4 is slightly forward. Bases of leaves should overlap one another to cover the holder completely. Leaf in Step 2 conceals base of flower stem.

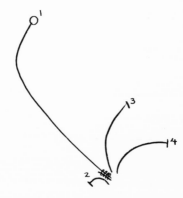

DESIGN 4

Irregular rising lines of bulrushes unite with furled aspidistra and Easter lilies in a celadon bowl.

Materials
1. 5 tall bulrushes
    Substitutes: Cattail or scouring rush
2. 3 aspidistra leaves (cast iron plant)
    Substitutes: Dracaena, ti, or bird's-nest fern
3. 2 Easter lilies
    Substitutes: Daylily, tiger lily, crinum lily, calla lily, or iris
4. 3"–4" needle-point holder
5. Round, oval, or square medium container
6. Pebbles

Method
Cut reeds in varying heights. Arrange them upright with a slight curve in each stem, all following the same direction. Reeds unite closely at the base. The three aspidistra leaves are also cut in different heights. Furl each leaf slightly as in pictured arrangement. Step 6 is partially in front of lower portion of reeds. Step 7 is slightly backward. Step 8 is slightly forward. Lower portion of leaves must unite at the base. Taller flower of Step 9 is to right of Step 6, with stem end behind the leaf. Shorter flower of Step 10 is leaning forward, with head turned inward, facing the taller flower. The stem end is behind leaf of Step 7. Cover holder with pebbles.

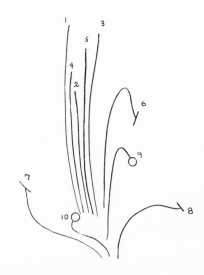

DESIGN 5

Stark torch lilies lend their fiery brilliance to the streaked ti leaves. The bronze bowl repeats the same rich tones of the exotic foliage.

Materials

1. 2 tall stems of torch lily
   Substitutes: Use bare, sturdy stems like lily-of-the-Nile, belladonna lily (amaryllis), anthurium, bird-of-paradise flower, or ginger
2. 3 ti leaves
   Substitutes: Aspidistra (cast iron plant), dracaena, or foliage of substitute flowers
3. 3"–4" needle-point holder
4. Round, square, or oval medium container
5. Pebbles

Method

The curves of this simple study move in a continuous rhythm. Note how the shortest leaf leads the eye to the other two leaves, and then up to the flowers and back to the inward furled tip. To achieve a similar rhythm, furl leaves as in the pictured arrangement. Step 1 is slightly forward with tip toward left. Step 2 overlaps lower portions of steps 1 and 3; its tip forms a loose furl. Tip of furled leaf in Step 3 turns inward. Base of leaves forms a semicircle around the flowers. Taller flower of Step 4 is upright, with a slight curve. Shorter flower of Step 5 curves inward to complete the rhythm of design. Cover holder with pebbles.

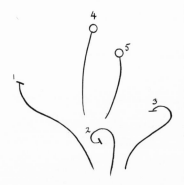

DESIGN 6

The lateral sweep of a rugged mountain pine branch, balanced by shorter pine, provides strength and character to the slender, rising lines of paper-white narcissus and their blades. Strength in the design is further emphasized by the dark bronze bowl.

Materials

1. 1 long pine branch and 2 or 3 shorter ones
2. 2 tall stems of narcissus
   Substitutes: Use other varieties of narcissus—daffodil or jonquil—or slender iris
3. 3–4 narcissus blades
   Substitutes: Leaves of substitute flower
4. 3″–4″ needle-point holder
5. Round or oval medium container

Method

Trim long pine branch to resemble pictured arrangement. Note how the bare parts of the branch reveal the rugged character of pine. Use the diagram as a guide for the movement of lines. The long, lateral sweep of Step 1 is slightly forward. Step 2 is also slightly forward, toward the right. Step 3 leans forward, toward the left, following Step 1. The taller flower is upright in the center behind the branches. Leaf of Step 5 is in front of flower, and Step 6 is partially behind Step 5. Step 7 is slightly forward, with flower head turned inward, facing the taller flower. Leaf of Step 8 is in front of Step 7. The three leaves unite at the base. Add short pine to cover rest of the holder.

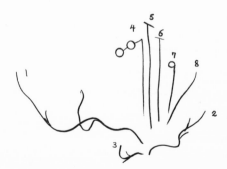

84

DESIGN 7

The broad leathery leaves of perforated monstera provide dynamic contrast to the sharp lines of cattails. This stark modern study is in a brown pottery container, tinged with yellow streaks.

Materials
1. 3 cattails
   Substitutes: Sturdy tall reeds or rushes
2. 2 monstera leaves (split-leaf philodendron)
   Substitutes: Any broad foliage of philodendron or rubber plant
3. 3″–4″ needle-point holder
4. Medium container with stem base
5. Pebbles

Method
Cut cattails in irregular heights. Bend steps 2 and 3 as pictured. (Bending will not cause a break if fresh cattails are used.) Step 1 is upright. Step 2 is slightly forward, toward left. Step 3 is close to Step 2. Taller leaf of Step 4 is toward left, in front of cattails. Leaf of Step 5 is in front of Step 4, slightly toward right. Lower portion of leaf brushes lightly over rim of container. Cover holder with pebbles.

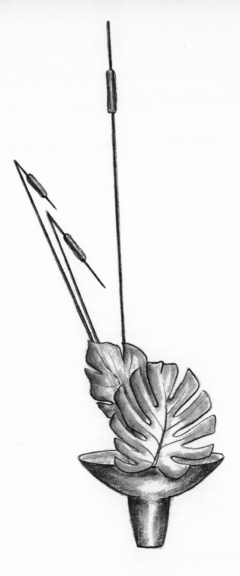

Yellow stalks of gladioli with their slender leaves form a simple double arrangement in a set of medium and small brown pottery bowls.

Materials

1.   3–4 stalks of gladioli (sword lily)
     Substitutes: Iris, narcissus, or belladonna lily (amaryllis)
2.   8–10 gladiolus leaves
     Substitutes: Leaves of substitute flower
3.   2 needle-point holders: 3″–4″ (medium), 2″–3″ (small)
4.   Different types of containers can be used for this design: Pair of round, square or oval; medium with small, in similar shapes or complementary; large, oval, or rectangle
5.   Pebbles

Method
Remove most of the leaves from flower stems. Diagram shows some leaves are left on flower stem. These can be removed and regrouped close to the flower to achieve a similar effect. Water-join leaves to keep them intact. Follow diagram for leaf groupings.

Left group. Tallest flower of Step 1 is slightly backward, and its leaf groupings are to the right of stem. Step 2 is slightly forward to the left of Step 1. Step 3 is also slightly forward, toward the right. Its degree of slant is beyond Step 2.

Right group. Flower of Step 1 is slightly backward. Budded stem of Step 2 is slightly forward. Leaf of Step 3 is partially in front of Step 2 and rises over larger bowl to unite the double grouping. Step 4 is placed close to side of Step 2. Note how leaves merge together at the base and give the impression of natural growth. The slight twist given some of the leaves softens the appearance of the rigid flowers.

Cover holders with pebbles.

Weeping willow spreads its wispy branches over two white Japanese irises enveloped by their strap blades. This tranquil water scene is enhanced by the sampan container of pale green porcelain.

Materials

1. Weeping willow
   Substitute: Corkscrew willow
2. 2 irises and 5 blades
   Substitutes: Narcissus, miniature calla lily, or brandy bottle
3. 3″–4″ needle-point holder
4. If boat container is unavailable, use oval or rectangular medium container
5. Pebbles

Method

The Japanese regard willow, narcissus, calla lily, and Japanese iris as water plants. Whatever materials are used they should reflect a waterside study. The willow branch must be tall enough, with a sturdy trunk to symbolize a tree. Trim to make wispy lines spread over flowers and foliage. (If umbrella palm is used cut stalks in uneven heights and arrange upright close together to symbolize a single growing plant.) The willow branch is inclined at a slant, slightly backward. The taller flower is upright, and the shorter one slightly forward, toward left. The strap leaves encircle the flower stems and branch. Tallest leaf of Step 6 is behind taller flower. Back of leaves face front in steps 3, 4, and 7 to emphasize the manner of their growth. Cover holder with pebbles, with a few drifting into the open water.

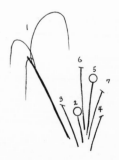

DESIGN   10

A spire of dark brown sea oats creates rich textural
harmony with cecropia leaves in this permanent dried
arrangement. The modern container is variegated brown
pottery.

Materials
1.   3 tall sprays of sea oats
     Substitutes: Tall sprays of dock, wheat, barley,
     or pampas grass
2.   2 cecropia leaves
     Substitutes: Dried cockscomb or clustered heads
     of yarrow
3.   3″–4″ needle-point holder, or mound of clay
4.   Container with stem base
5.   Pebbles

Method
Cut sprays of sea oats in irregular heights. Arrange them
upright in the needle-point holder or mound of clay.
Taller cecropia leaf of Step 4 is slightly forward, and the
shorter one of Step 5 is in front of the sea oats. Cover
holder with pebbles. Color of pebbles should not detract
from the floral materials. Use dark brown tones to blend
in with sea oats.

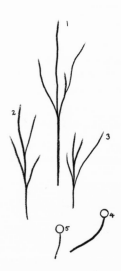

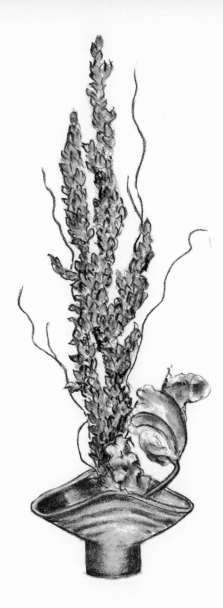

93

DESIGN   11

Looped blades of New Zealand flax form the framework of this modern centerpiece, with low clusters of
kafir lilies centered in an oval black porcelain bowl.

Materials
1. 6 blades of New Zealand flax
    Substitutes: Screw pine (pandanus), dracaena or
    any sturdy strap blades
2. 3–4 clusters of kafir lilies
    Substitutes: Clusters of narcissus, hydrangea, or
    geranium; 6–7 single flowers of carnation, tulip,
    gardenia or jasmine
3. 3″–4″ needle-point holder
4. Florist wire
5. Round or oval medium bowl

Method
This practical centerpiece can vary from large to small
without losing the appeal of the design. Cut leaves in
varying heights. Loop each leaf with tip meeting base,
and tie with florist wire. Steps 1–6 are inserted in a semicircle, leaving sufficient room in the center for the flowers. Cut flower stems short and group closely together,
with some blossoms brushing lightly over rim of container. This design has an all-round perspective. Fill in
with additional short blossoms if holder is still visible.

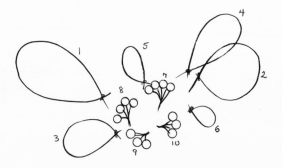

Pussy willows form a flowing outline for daffodils and their leaves. A small grouping of mignonettes completes the double woodland in a brown porcelain container.

Materials

1. 4 long pussy willow stems
   Substitutes: Broom, corkscrew willow, weeping willow, or weeping birch
2. 3 daffodils and 9 strap leaves
   Substitutes: Use any variety of narcissus or iris with blades of same flower
3. 3 mignonettes
   Substitutes: Button chrysanthemum, aster, daisy, or wild pink
4. 2 needle-point holders: 3"–4" (medium), 2"–3" (small)
5. Oval or rectangular large container
6. Pebbles

Method

Cut willow stems in varying heights. Curve each line similarly to pictured arrangement. Step 1 is slightly backward. Step 2 is slightly forward. Step 3 is slightly backward, beyond Step 1. Step 4 is slanting forward. Leave sufficient space between steps 3 and 4 to arrange the flowers and foliage. Flower of Step 5 is slightly backward. Group three leaves close to stem. Diagram shows how leaves should appear in front of flower stem. Step 6 is slightly forward, close to Step 4. Group three leaves to cover part of flower stem and willow. Step 7 is leaning forward with flower head turned inward. Group three leaves to cover lower part of willow and flower stem. Cover holder sparingly with pebbles, allowing some to drift into the open water.

Arrange a small grouping of three to five mignonettes to far right of container. Step 1 is slightly backward; Step 2 is slightly forward; Step 3 is leaning backward. Cover holder with additional leaves.

97

DESIGN 13

Rich copper tones of ti leaves, arranged in a brown pottery bowl, make a striking foliage study.

Materials

1. 7 ti leaves
   Substitutes: Aspidistra (cast iron plant) or dracaena
2. 3"–4" needle-point holder
3. Oval or round medium bowl
4. Pebbles

Method

Cut leaves in irregular heights. The tallest leaf of Step 1 is at a backward slant. Step 2 is behind Step 1. Make tight furls for steps 3–7. Steps 3, 4, and 5 rise in graduated heights and are slightly backward. Steps 6 and 7 are in a tight cluster in front of steps 1 and 2. Cover holder with pebbles.

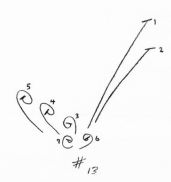

DESIGN 14

An imaginary woodland is created with dracaena, daisy-chrysanthemums, and mugo pine in half-moon containers of green porcelain.

Materials

1. 5 dracaena leaves
   Substitutes: Ti, aspidistra (cast iron plant), or bird's-nest fern
2. 3–4 sprigs of short pine
   Substitutes: Any small leafy shrub like boxwood
3. 3–5 sprays of daisy-chrysanthemums
   Substitutes: Use flowers to suggest a woodland—aster, marigold, daisy, zinnia—or flowering shrubs like azalea, bouvardia, or daphne
4. 2 needle-point holders, 3"–4" each
5. Different containers can be used for this design: A pair of similar containers as pictured, or rectangular; large round or square container; large oval or rectangular container
6. Pebbles

Method

Left group: Cut leaves in varying heights. Furl steps 3, 4, and 5 as pictured. Longest leaf of Step 1, with slight twist, is slanting backward. Furled leaf of Step 2 is slightly backward, with tip facing inward. Step 3 is leaning forward. Furled leaf of Step 4 is in the center with tip facing longest leaf. The short leaf of Step 5 is between steps 2 and 3. Add short sprigs of pine to encircle the leaves in steps 2, 3, and 5. Cover holder with pebbles, with some drifting into the open water.

Right group: Cut flower stems in varying heights. Form a low triangle with steps 1, 2, and 3. Step 1 is slanting forward. Step 2 is slanting backward. Step 3 is leaning backward, reaching into the other container to complete the unity of design. Add short foliage of the flowers to cover the holder completely.

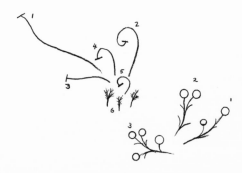

DESIGN 15

Asparagus ferns swirl around three yellow hybrid roses in an emerald-green porcelain vase.

Materials

1. 2 long asparagus ferns
   Substitutes: Similar soft fern or vines—wisteria, bittersweet, woodbine, or ivy
2. 3 roses
   Substitutes: Carnation, daylily, Easter lily, Japanese lily, or cattleya orchid
3. Y-shaped support
4. Vase of medium height

Method

Place support in vase. Arrange two long stems of ferns or vines to form a rhythmic framework for the flowers. Step 1 is slightly backward. Step 2 is slightly forward. If roses are used, trim leaves to create a similar airy feeling. Flower of Step 3 is slightly backward. Step 4 is slanting backward. Step 5 is leaning forward, toward left, with some leaves brushing lightly over rim of vase. If flowers have no leaves of their own, add short sprays of fern, or substitute material, around the stems.

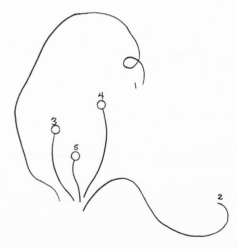

Bushy heads of lily-leeks merge in harmonious textures with narrow New Zealand flax. The tall pottery container of variegated brown-yellow tones highlights this modern study.

Materials

1. 3 long blades of New Zealand flax
    Substitutes: Striped dracaena, screw pine (pandanus), leaves of belladonna lily (amaryllis) or lily-of-the-Nile, or sturdy ribbed grass blades
2. 2 stalks of lily-leeks
    Substitutes: Queen Anne's lace flower, lily-of-the-Nile, belladonna lily, or torch lily
3. 3″–4″ needle-point holder
4. Tall similarly shaped container with closed bowl top
5. Pebbles

Method

Flower of Step 1 is slightly backward with curved stalk facing inward. The natural twist in the shorter flower gives a note of interest to the design. For variation of this line, cut flower of Step 2 short, and place it slanting forward with the stem end behind the taller flower. Curve leaves of steps 3 and 4 as pictured; arrange to sweep across the tall flower. Step 3 is in front of Step 1. Step 4 is behind Step 3. The tallest leaf of Step 5 is behind tall flower. Curve tip of leaf slightly to turn inward. Cover holder with pebbles.

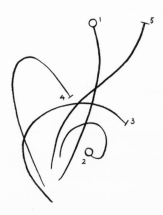

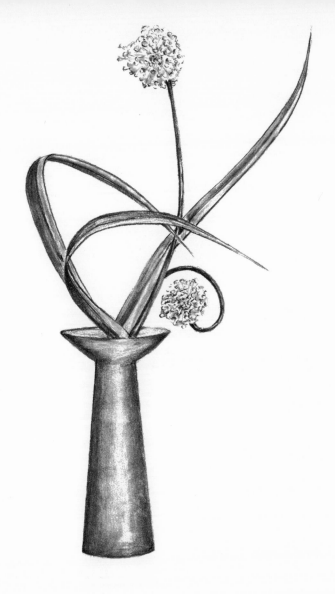

Snowdrops with their slender leaves grace a hollowed bamboo container in a natural arrangement.

Materials
1.   2 snowdrops with long stems
      Substitutes: Narcissus, iris, Peruvian lily, scarborough lily, swamp lily (crinum), or lady slipper
2.   7 leaves of snowdrops
      Substitutes: Slender blades of substitute flower or sturdy grass blades
3.   Cross support
4.   Florist wire
5.   Vase with front opening or a standard vase of medium height

Method
Place cross support in vase. Taller flower of Step 1 is slightly backward. Group two long leaves and place in front of Step 1. (Diagram shows the natural leaves on the stems of the flowers.) Step 2 is slanting forward with flower facing the taller one. Group two leaves and place in front of Step 2. Group three leaves and place in front of steps 1 and 2. Note how leaves in the design form a close union at the base and spread out in a free-flowing feeling. To keep leaves intact, water-join them.

Thin wire tied loosely around the base of leaves will also hold them securely.

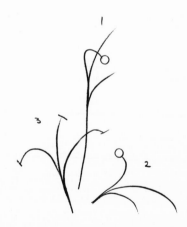

107

Tall stalks of Formosan reeds, combined with yellow spider chrysanthemums, make a natural vase study. The slender container is brown pottery set on a natural wood base.

Materials

1. 4 tall stalks of similar reeds
   Substitute: Hardy bamboo
2. 2 chrysanthemums
   Substitutes: Aster, zinnia, windflower (anemone), rose, or marigold
3. **Y**-support
4. Tall, narrow, medium vase
5. Oval or rectangular base (optional)

Method

Place **Y**-support in vase. Trim reeds to resemble sparse foliage distribution as in pictured arrangement. The clean lines of partially bare stalks give emphasis to the design. Step 1 is slightly backward. Make sharp bend in stalk of Step 2 to suggest realism of natural growth. Insert toward left with downward part of stalk facing toward right, in front of Step 1. Step 3 is slightly forward, toward right. Step 4 is slightly forward, toward left. Taller flower is slightly backward, and the shorter one is slightly forward. Trim heavy leaves of the flowers. Lip of vase should be lightly covered with foliage. If a base is used, set vase off center for spatial balance.

Pussy willows, yellow Dutch irises, and cypress form a modern design. Smooth black pebbles, scattered at the base, add visual balance to the double cylindrical container of black porcelain.

Materials

1. 2 long pussy willow stems
   Substitutes: Broom, corkscrew willow, or slender juniper
2. 2 irises with their foliage
   Substitutes: Narcissus, tulip, tiger lily, or orchid, with foliage
3. 5 short sprays of cypress
   Substitutes: Mugo pine, box, or a flowering shrub like andromeda or azalea
4. 2 Y-supports
5. 2 narrow cylindrical vases of different heights may be substituted for this unusual container
6. Black pebbles or a color to harmonize with selected containers

Method

The willow, or substitute material, must be fresh for this design. The loop can only be made with supple material. The taller willow, with a slight curve, is placed upright in support in taller vase. This is Step 1. Make a hook with shorter willow for Step 2, as pictured. Insert slightly forward. Taller flower of Step 3 is upright in support in shorter vase. Step 4 is slightly forward. Add short sprays of cypress, or substitute foliage, to cover lightly rims of the vases. Note how clusters unite the double arrangement. Scatter pebbles at the base.

Bleached wisteria branches and buff artichoke heads united with blue skyrockets in a modern dried arrangement. The twisted porcelain vase is deep blue.

Materials

1. 2 dried artichoke heads (known commercially as cordone puffs)
   Substitutes: Lily-leek, hydrangea, or cockscomb
2. 2 wisteria branches
3. 4–5 clusters of skyrockets
   Substitutes: Small strawflowers
4. Y-shaped support
5. Florist wire
6. Vase of medium height

Method

Dried wisteria branches, if soaked in water for several hours, will become supple enough to be bent into appealing forms. Form a continuous rhythmic movement with the two wisteria branches as shown in steps 1 and 2 of the diagram. Insert securely in the support. Cut artichoke stems in extreme heights. The shorter flower of Step 3 is slightly forward, and the taller one of Step 4 is behind it, slanting forward. Tie small clusters of skyrockets with florist wire. Insert three to four clusters behind shorter flower for depth, and a small cluster between the two flowers.

This quiet classical study of bird's-nest ferns blends harmoniously with the dark copper container.

Materials

1. 7 bird's-nest ferns
    Substitutes: Dracaena, ti, or wild anthurium foliage
2. 3"–4" needle-point holder
3. Square, round, or oval medium container
4. Pebbles

Method

The leaves for this design must be firm, fresh, and long. If some leaves are torn or bruised, trim them by cutting along the margin of the leaf. Apply the same technique in grading some of the leaves for the design. Follow lines in the diagram.

Measurements for the three radical lines: Principal: 3½ times length of this medium container; Secondary: Half of Principal; Tertiary: One-third of Principal.

Relative measurements and placement of foliage in relation to the three radical lines:

Step 1: Half of Secondary. Back of leaf faces front. Insert toward left, slightly forward.

Step 2: Secondary line. Insert behind Step 1, slanting forward.

Step 3: Half of Principal. Back of leaf faces front. Insert upright behind Step 1.

Step 4: Tertiary line. Insert toward right, slanting backward.

Step 5: Half of Tertiary. Insert in curve of Step 4 leaf, slanting backward.

Step 6: Principal line. Insert upright with slight curve of stem facing right, toward the Tertiary line.

Step 7: A little below height of Principal. Insert close to left of Principal, with curve of leaf partially encircling the Principal.

Cover holder with pebbles. This is a right-hand form of the Formal Seika style.

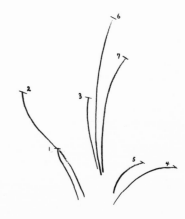

Red tulips and their leaves make a dramatic classical study in a black porcelain bowl.

Materials

1. 3 tulips and 8 leaves
   Substitutes: Barberton daisy (gerberia), calla lilies, belladonna lily (amaryllis), or Japanese iris, with foliage
2. 3″–4″ needle-point holder
3. Round, oval, or square medium container
4. Pebbles

Method

Flowers should be selected in different stages of development. A bud for Step 6, a partially opened flower for Step 8, and an open flower for Step 10. The leaves are an expressive part of this classical design. Separate most of them from the flower stems. Select the best leaves for the lines of steps 2, 5, and 11. Trim all torn or bruised leaves.

Measurements for the three radical lines: Principal: 2½ times diameter of this medium container; Secondary: Half of Principal; Tertiary: One-third of Principal.

Relative measurements and placement of leaves and flowers in relation to the three radical lines:

Step 1: Half of Secondary. Back of leaf faces front. Insert toward left, slightly forward.

Step 2: Secondary line. Insert behind Step 1, slanting forward.

Step 3: Three-fourths of Secondary. Back of leaf faces front. Insert upright behind Step 1.

Step 4: Slightly taller than Step 3. Insert toward left, behind Step 3.

Step 5: Tertiary line. Insert toward right, slanting backward.

Step 6: One-third of Principal. Insert in curve of Step 5 leaf.

Step 7: Three-fourths of Tertiary. Insert behind Step 6.

Step 8: One-half of Principal. Insert upright, behind Step 3.

Step 9: Three-fourths of Principal. Insert upright, behind Step 8.

Step 10: Principal. Insert upright with slight curve of stem facing right, toward the Tertiary line. Tip is directly above base.

Step 11: A little below height of Principal. Insert close to left of Principal, with curve of leaf partially encircling the Principal.

Cover holder with pebbles. This is a right-hand form of the Formal Seika style.

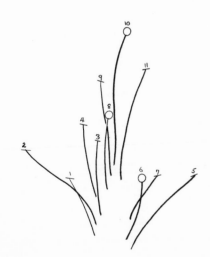

117

Young pine shoots form the Principal and Secondary lines of this classical study; with pink camellias and their sturdy foliage for the Tertiary line. The rough textures of the weathered wood container add finishing touches to the harmonious relationships in the design.

Materials

1. 5 sturdy pine branches
   Substitutes: Yew, juniper, or broom
2. 2–3 camellia branches with a few blossoms
   Substitutes: Chrysanthemum, peony, small dahlia, or rose
3. 3″–4″ needle-point holder
4. Oval or rectangular medium container
5. Rock of irregular shape or pebbles

Method

If pine branches are used, the needles must be firm in order to give the design strength and character. Trim branches to achieve clean lines but with some sprouting shoots. When curving each line make sure the base is straight from 3″–4″ high, and all lower part of foliage removed. Follow lines in the diagram. Leaves should appear sparingly on camellia branches, with two or three flowers in varying stages of development.

Measurements for the three radical lines: Principal: 2½ times length of this medium container; Secondary: Half of Principal; Tertiary: One-third of Principal.

Relative measurements and placement of branches in relation to the three radical lines:

Step 1: Secondary line. Insert toward left, slanting forward.

Step 2: Half of Secondary. Insert behind Step 1, slanting backward.

Step 3: Tertiary line. Insert toward right, slanting backward.

Step 4: Half of Tertiary. Insert behind Step 3 but curving forward over Step 3.

Step 5: Principal line. Insert upright with curve of branch facing right, toward the Tertiary line.

Step 6: Three-fourths of Principal. Place close to left of Principal.

Step 7: Half of Principal. Place close to right of Principal.

Cover holder with rock or pebbles. This is a right-hand form of the Formal Seika style.

119

DESIGN 24

Scotch broom and pink peonies merge harmoniously in a classical study. The smooth porcelain modern container is jet black.

Materials

1. 4–5 branches of Scotch broom
   Substitutes: Pussy willow, yew, pine, juniper, or slender flowering branches—mock orange, bridal wreath, cherry, or golden bells (forsythia)
2. 3 peonies (small)—see comment below
   Substitutes: Chrysanthemum, rose, dahlia, or iris
3. 3″–4″ needle-point holder
4. Similar container, or round, oval or square medium container
5. Pebbles

Method

This classical design may also be composed of all green foliage or flowering branches. In this instance, use three additional lines to replace the flowers. When curving each line make sure the base is straight from 3″–4″ high, and all lower part of foliage is removed. Follow lines in the diagram. All lines must merge together at the base to symbolize a single growing plant. If flowers are used they should vary in stages of development from bud to mature flower.

Measurements for the three radical lines: Principal: Approximately eight times height of this modern container, or about three times diameter of medium shallow container; Secondary: Half of Principal; Tertiary: One-third of Principal.

Relative measurements and placement of branches and flowers in relation to the three radical lines:

Step 1: Secondary line. Insert toward right, slanting forward.

Step 2: Tertiary line. Insert toward left, slanting backward.

Step 3: Three-fourths of Tertiary. Insert behind Step 2.

Step 4: Principal line. Insert upright with curve of branch facing left, toward the Tertiary line.

Step 5: Little less than half of Principal. Place behind Step 1 with upper portion of leaves and flower head facing forward.

Step 6: Little less than half of Principal. Place close to left of Principal.

Step 7: Half of Tertiary. Place close to Step 2.

Cover holder with pebbles. This is a left-hand form of the Formal Seika style.

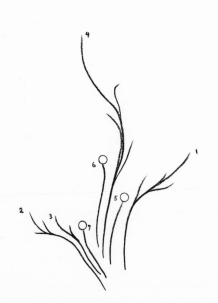

121

Appendix
Popular Plants Used in Flower Arrangement

No attempt is made here to cover the plant kingdom, which consists of over 350,000 species and additional thousands of subspecies and varieties. This general classification is given primarily to assist the flower arranger in identifying the different generic types of popular plants used in flower arrangement. Since the common names of plants vary considerably, Latin botanical terms are also given.*

BREAKDOWN OF CLASSIFICATION

TREES: Evergreen and deciduous.

SHRUBS: Woody plants of bushy habit—flowering, nonflowering, and those which bear berries.

FOLIAGE PLANTS: Includes all kinds of ferns and leaves of flowerless plants.

VINES: All kinds of climbing plants and also certain shrubs with long flexible roots.

FLOWERS: This category of nonwoody (herbaceous) plants is so numerous that only the most popular names can be mentioned.

ORNAMENTAL GRASSES AND SWAMP HERBS: Members of the grass and sedge families which have decorative forms of plumelike clusters and spikes.

* Source: L. H. Bailey and Ethel Zoe Bailey, *Hortus Second*, New York, The Macmillan Company, 1941.

TREES, SHRUBS, FOLIAGE PLANTS

Aspidistra. See CAST IRON PLANT.	
African pine	*Podocarpus*
Arbor-vitae	*Thuja*
Asparagus fern	{ *Asparagus plumosus* / *As. sprengerii*
Australian pine	*Araucaria*
Azalea	*Rhododendron*
Baby's breath	*Gypsophila*
Bird's-nest fern	*Asplenium nidus*
Bog arum	*Calla palustris*
Boxwood	*Buxus*
Brake fern	*Pteris serrulata*
Bridal wreath	*Spiraea*
California poppy	*Eschscholtzia californica*
Cast iron plant	*Aspidistra*
Cedar	{ *Cupressus* / *Juniperus* / *Cedrus*
Ceriman	*Monstera deliciosa*
Chinese peach	*Prunus persica*
Chinese pine	*Primula sinensis*
Chinese tree peony	*Paeonia suffruticosa*
Cotoneaster	*Cotoneaster*
Daphne	*Daphne*
Evergreen plant	*Aspidistra*
False spiraea	*Sorbaria*
Fir	*Abies*
Firethorn	*Pyracantha*

Flowering apple	*Malus floribunda*, etc.
Flowering dogwood	*Cornus florida*
Garden huckleberry	*Solanum nigrum*
Golden-bells	*Forsythia*
Hardy bamboo	*Pseudosasa*
Heavenly bamboo	*Nandina*
Holly	*Ilex*
Japanese pine	*Pittosporum tobira*
Japanese quince	*Chaenomeles lagenaria*
Japanese white pine	*Pinus parviflora*
Japanese yew	{ *Podocarpus macrophylla* / *Taxus cuspidata*
Japanese maple	*Acer palmatum*
Jasmine	*Jasminum*
Juniper	*Juniperus*
Lady's eardrops	*Fuchsia hybrida*
Acrostichum	*Laurel*
Leatherfern	*Laurus nobilis*
Leatherleaf philodendron	*Philodendron guttiferum*
Lilac	*Syringa vulgaris*
Lily of China	*Rohdea japonica*
Loquat	*Eryobotrya japonica*
Magnolia	{ *Magnolia campbellii* / *M. grandiflora* / *M. soulangeana*
Mimosa	*Acacia decurrens* var. *dealbata*
Mock orange	*Philadelphus, Murraea*
Mother-in-law tongue, Snake plant	*Sansevieria*
Mountain cypress	*Libocedrus bidwillii*

		VINES	
Mountain pine, mugo pine	*Pinus mugo*	American ivy	*Parthenocissus quinquefolia*
Nandina. See HEAVENLY BAMBOO.		Begonia tree vine	*Cissus discolor*
		Bittersweet	*Solanum dulcamara*
New Zealand flax	*Phormium tenax*	Boston ivy	*Parthenocissus tricuspidata*
Oregon grape	*Mahonia*	Bougainvillea	*Bougainvillea*
Peach tree	*Prunus persica*	Climbing hydrangea	*Hydrangea petiolaris*
Privet	*Ligustrum*	Climbing rose	*Rosa banksiae*
Pussy willows	*Salix discolor*	English ivy	*Hedera helix*
Pygmy bamboo	*Sasa pygmaea*	Greenbrier	*Smilax*
Rhododendron	{ *Rhododendron maximum* / *R. macrophyllum* }	Hanging geranium	*Pelargonium peltatum*
		Honeysuckle	*Lonicera*
Screw pine	*Pandanus*	Japanese ivy	*Hedera helix var. conglomereta*
Scotch broom	*Cytisus scoparius*		
Snake plant	*Sansevieria*	Magnolia vine	*Schisandra*
Snow willow	*Spiraea thunbergii*	Morning glory	*Convolvulus, Ipomaea*
Snow-heather	*Erica carnea*	Nasturtium	*Tropaeolum*
Spanish broom	*Spartium junceum*	Passion flower	*Passiflora*
Spindle tree	*Euonymus japonicus*	Philodendron vine	*Philodendron*
Split-leaf philodendron, swiss cheese plant	*Monstera deliciosa*	Sweet pea	*Lathyrus odoratus*
		Woodbine	*Clematis virginiana*
Spruce	*Picea*		
Statice	*Limonium sinuatum*		
Strawberry bush	*Euonymus americanus*		
Striped dracaena	*Dracaena deremensis var., warneckii*	**FLOWERS**	
Sweet alyssum	*Alyssum maritimum*		
Ti	*Cordyline*		
Tree dahlia	*Dahlia imperialis*	African daisy	{ *Gerberia* / *Arctotis* (especially *A. stoechadifolia*) }
Weeping birch	*Betula pendula*		
Weeping willow	*Babylonica*		

African lily	*Agapanthus africanus*	Corn marigold	*Chrysanthemum*
Algerian iris	*Iris unguicularis*	Cyclamen	*Cyclamen persicum*
Amaryllis	*Hippeastrum*	Cymbidium orchid	*Cymbidium*
Amazon lily	*Eucharis grandiflora*	Daffodil	*Narcissus pseudo-narcissus*
Anemone. See WINDFLOWER.		Daisy	*Chrysanthemum frutescens*
Anthurium	*Anthurium andraeanum*	Daylily	*Hemerocallis*
Aster, annual	*Callistephus chinensis*	Dutch hyacinth	*Hyacinthus orientalis*
Bachelor button	*Centaurea cyanus*	Dutch iris 'Golden Harvest'	*Iris hybrid*
Barberton daisy	*Gerberia jamesonii*	Easter lily	*Lilium longiflorum*
Bearded iris	*Iris germanica hybrid*	Feverfew	*Chrysanthemum parthenium*
Beefsteak begonia	*Begonia feastii*	Florist's geranium	*Pelargonium*
Beefsteak geranium	{ *Saxifraga sarmentosa* / *Begonia rex-cultorum*	Garden dahlia	*Dahlia pinnata hybrid*
		Garden pompom 'Joybringer'	*Chrysanthemum*
Belladonna lily	*Amaryllis belladonna*	Gladiolus. See SWORD LILY.	
Bird-of-paradise flower	*Strelitzia*	Globe daisy	*Globularia trichosantha*
Blue lace-flower	*Trachymene caerulea*	Globe thistle	*Echinops*
Brandy bottle	*Nuphar lutea*	Gloxinia	*Sinningia speciosa*
Button snakeroot	*Liatrus*	Grape hyacinth	*Muscari*
California geranium	*Senecio petasitis*	Hyacinth	*Hyacinthus orientalis*
Calla lily	*Zantedeschia aethiopica*	(and see specific type, *e.g.*, DUTCH HYACINTH)	
Canna	*Canna generalis*		
Carnation	*Dianthus*	Hybrid perpetual rose	*Rosa borboniana hybrid*
Cattleya orchid	*Cattleya labiata*	Hybrid tea rose	*Rosa odorata hybrid*
China aster	*Callistephus chinensis*	Iris	
China rose	{ *Hibiscus rosa-sinensis* / *Rosa chinensis*	(and see specific type, *e.g.*, MOURNING IRIS)	
		Japanese iris	{ *Iris kaempferi* / *J. laevigata*
Chinese sacred lily	*Narcissus tazetta*		
Chrysanthemum	*Chrysanthemum*	Japanese lily	*Lilium speciosum*
(and see specific type, *e.g.*, CORN MARIGOLD)		Jonquil	*Narcissus jonquilla*
Cockscomb	*Celosia*	Kafir lily	{ *Schizostylis* / *Clivia*
Columbine	*Aquilegia*		

Lady slipper	{ Cypripedium { Paphiopedilum	Queen Anne's lace	Daucus
Lake iris	Iris lacustris	Roof iris	Iris tectorum
Lily-of-the-Nile	Agapanthus africanus	Rose	Rosa
Lily-of-the-valley	Convallaria majalis	(and see specific type, *e.g.*,	
Lily-leek	Allium moly	HYBRID TEA ROSE)	
Madonna lily	Lilium candidum		
Marguerite	Chrysanthemum frutescens	Royal lily	Lilium regale
Marigold	Tagetes	Sacred lily of China	Rohdea
Michaelmas daisy	Aster	Scarborough lily	Vallota
Mignonette	Reseda odorata	Shasta daisy	Chrysanthemum maximum
Miniature calla	Callopsis volkensis	Siberian lily	Ixiolirion tataricum
Mourning iris	Iris susiana	Sky-flower	Duranta repens
Mum	Chrysanthemum morifolium	Snapdragon	Antirrhinum
	hortorum	Snowdrop	Galanthus nivalis
		Spider Mum 'Bridesmaid'	Chrysanthemum
Oleander	Nerium	Sunflower	Helianthus
One-day lily	Tigridia	Swamp lily	Crinum
Orchid amaryllis	Sprekelia formosissima	Sweet William	Dianthus barbatus
Orchid cactus	Epiphyllum	Sword lily	Gladiolus
Oriental poppy	Papaver orientale	Torch lily	Kniphofia
Paper-white narcissus	Narcissus tazetta	Transvaal daisy	Gerberia jamesonii
Paris daisy	Chrysanthemum frutescens	Tulip	Tulipa
Peony	Paeonia	Tuberose	Polianthes tuberosa
Peruvian lily	Alstroemeria	Tuberous begonia	Begonia tuberhybrida
Petticoat daffodil	Narcissus bulbocodium	Water arum (bog arum)	Calla palustris
Petunia	Petunia	Water lily	Nymphaea
Phlox	Polemoniaceae	Water lotus	Nelumbium
Pink	Dianthus	Windflower	Anemone
Plantain lily	Hosta	Wood hyacinth	Scilla
Poet's narcissus	Narcissus poeticus	Woodland orchid	Orchis spectabilis
Poker plant	Kniphofia	Yarrow	Achillea
Primrose	Primula	Zinnia	Zinnia elegans

Bamboo	*Arundinaria* *Bambusa* *Sasa, etc.*
Barley	*Hordeum*
Beard grass	*Andropogon orgenteus*
Brome grass	*Bromus*
Bulrush	*Scirpus*
Cane reed	*Arundinaria gigantea*
Cattail	*Acalypha*
Eulalia	*Miscanthus sinensis*
Feather grass	*Stipa pennata*
Fountain grass	*Pennisetum ruppeli*
Giant reed	*Arundo donax*
Horsetail	*Equisetum*
Miscanthus	*Miscanthus sinensis*
Palm grass	*Setaria palmifolia*
Pampas grass	*Cortaderia*
Papyrus	*Cyperus papyrus*
Ribbon grass	*Phalaris arundinacea var. picta*
Scouring rush	*Equisetum*
Spike grass	*Uniola*
Sea oats	*Uniola paniculata*
Zebra grass	*Miscanthus sinensis var. zebrinus*